Building Wealth

Mastering the Art of Investing in Emerging Neighborhoods

By
Nathan Venture, D

To You,

Thank You!

Contents

Introduction:
The Lure of Emerging Neighborhoods

For a seasoned investor or a newcomer eyeing the next big opportunity, emerging neighborhoods represent a tantalizing prospect. The allure of these areas lies not just in their potential for handsome returns, but also in the dynamic interplay of progress, community transformation, and sometimes, a complete overhaul of urban identity. In emerging neighborhoods, change is the only constant, and savvy investors who understand how to ride this wave stand to benefit immensely.

So, what makes emerging neighborhoods so compelling? The appeal isn't merely surface-deep; it's grounded in solid economic principles, societal shifts, and infrastructural advancements. Investing in these areas at the right time can yield substantial profits, often outperforming more established markets. It's not merely about jumping on a trend but understanding the various elements that contribute to a neighborhood's growth.

One of the biggest attractions of emerging neighborhoods is affordability coupled with potential. Established neighborhoods often come with high price tags and moderated growth rates. In contrast, emerging neighborhoods offer investors the opportunity to buy low with the prospect of selling high. But it's not about cheap prices—it's about value and foresight. Recognizing the foundational elements that signal future growth is key.

Consider the role of *infrastructure development*. New transport links, schools, commercial centers, and parks often precede or coincide with a neighborhood's rise. These infrastructural changes act as both a cause and effect of neighborhood progress, attracting businesses and residents alike. The subsequent uptick in demand usually leads to appreciation in property values, providing excellent returns for those who invested early.

Demographics also play a vital role. Shifts in population dynamics, such as an influx of younger residents or an increase in disposable incomes, can transform the social fabric and consumer base of a neighborhood. Understanding these shifts requires not just data but keen insight into the qualitative aspects of community life.

Another key driver is the entrepreneurial spirit. Emerging neighborhoods often become hotspots for startups and small businesses, bringing vitality and innovation to these areas. The introduction of trendy cafes, boutique shops, and co-working spaces not only serves the local community but also adds to the area's attractiveness, fueling further investment.

However, it's not just about identifying the right neighborhood; it's about timing and strategy. Some markets may show promise but lack the immediate fundamentals necessary for short-term gains. Others may be ripe for quick returns but limited in long-term potential. Balancing these factors requires both skill and strategic planning.

In the pages that follow, we'll explore these aspects in greater depth, providing you with actionable insights and proven strategies to navigate and conquer the complex landscape of emerging neighborhoods. We'll delve into the basics of understanding market conditions, supply and demand dynamics, as well as how to evaluate a neighborhood's growth potential. The aim is to equip you with the knowledge to pinpoint opportunities, mitigate risks, and ultimately, build a robust investment portfolio.

Investing in emerging neighborhoods also carries an added layer of social responsibility. While the goal is to maximize returns, it's crucial to consider the community's well-being. Ethical investing and enhancing community value should be part of your broader strategy. When done correctly, these investments can uplift not just your financial standing but also the lives of residents, contributing to a more equitable and prosperous urban future.

As we journey through this guide, seasoned investors will find reaffirmation and refinement of their strategies, while newcomers will gain valuable foundations to build upon. We'll discuss how to effectively analyze market conditions, understand the long-term impacts of government policies, and utilize cutting-edge technology to sharpen your investment acumen. Additionally, we'll uncover hidden gems within the commercial real estate sector and analyze the intricate balance of building a diversified portfolio.

The exploration of emerging neighborhoods isn't just about financial gain; it's about recognizing and participating in the transformative processes that shape cities and communities. It's about tapping into the pulse of progress and aligning your investments with the inevitable march of development.

Emerging neighborhoods are not static—they're living, evolving entities. And as we navigate this landscape, remember that the key to success lies in informed, strategic, and responsible investing. Let's embark on this journey to uncover opportunities that could not only transform your financial portfolio but also contribute positively to the communities and cities of tomorrow.

Welcome to the world of emerging neighborhoods, where the future is ready for those prepared to seize it.

Chapter 1:
Building Wealth: Mastering the Art of Investing in Emerging Neighborhoods

Investing in real estate, particularly in emerging neighborhoods, presents unique opportunities for creating long-term wealth. But what's an emerging neighborhood, and why should investors turn their attention to these areas? An emerging neighborhood is a region experiencing economic growth, infrastructure development, and demographic shifts, making it ripe for investment. By identifying these spots before they hit the mainstream, investors can get ahead of the curve, capturing value and capitalizing on substantial appreciation in property values.

Emerging neighborhoods didn't always have the best reputation. Often, they're in transition, evolving from underdeveloped or underserved areas. But that's precisely what creates the opportunity. Think of these investments not as risky gambles but as calculated strategies. The initial phases might bring challenges; however, with diligent research and sensible planning, the financial upside is significant. For those willing to dive in, the rewards can be profound.

So, why do emerging neighborhoods hold so much potential? These areas are usually subject to changing dynamics driven by various factors such as new businesses moving in, young professionals seeking affordable living spaces, or local governments investing in infrastructure improvements. When you spot these indicators early, you position yourself at the forefront of a trend that can multiply your investment returns exponentially.

Let's break this down further. Consider the scenario where a new tech company announces its intention to build a campus in a part of town that has been long overlooked. What follows is a ripple effect: new jobs, higher demand for housing, and subsequently, increased property values. The key is recognizing these patterns before they are fully visible to the broader market.

When we discuss emerging neighborhoods, we're not merely talking about immediate financial gain. Sure, quick gains are possible, but the real beauty lies in long-term wealth creation. Think of investing in emerging neighborhoods as planting seeds for trees that will bear fruit season after season. This strategy allows you to steadily build a portfolio that appreciates over time, providing a stable financial foundation.

But how does one start investing in such areas? The first step involves comprehensive market analysis. Look at trends related to demographic changes, economic indicators, crime rates, and amenities like schools and parks. Neighborhoods showing consistent improvement in these areas are prime targets. When you combine this data with boots-on-the-ground research, such as talking to local residents and business owners, you gain invaluable insights that can guide your investment choices.

Another essential aspect is understanding the role of infrastructure. Significant projects like new transit lines, highway expansions, or public space enhancements can drastically alter a neighborhood's appeal. When city planners allocate funds to improve public transport or build new recreational facilities, they're signaling their confidence in the area's future growth. As an investor, paying attention to these signals allows you to align your investments with the direction of planned growth.

Timing is also crucial. Jumping in too late means you'll pay a premium, reducing your potential returns. On the other hand, too early an entry can tie up capital in an area where the improvement timeline doesn't match your investment horizon. Striking the right balance requires not just data but also intuition and experience.

Consider engaging with local real estate professionals who specialize in emerging neighborhoods. Their in-depth knowledge of the local market can offer you a competitive edge. These experts are often privy to developments and shifts that aren't yet public knowledge. Leveraging their expertise allows you to move swiftly and confidently.

It's equally important to diversify within this niche. Don't put all your eggs in one basket by investing in a single emerging neighborhood. Instead, look for multiple areas that show promise. This way, you're not overly exposed to the risks associated with any single market. Diversification spreads your risk while still positioning you to capture gains from several rising areas.

Of course, engaging with any investment comes with its own set of risks. The key to successful investing in emerging neighborhoods lies in risk management. Mitigate risks by thoroughly vetting properties, conducting environmental assessments, and being aware of zoning laws and other regulatory concerns. Evaluating these factors can prevent unforeseen issues that might affect your investment's profitability.

Another layer of risk management involves staying financially flexible. Secure adequate financing, but also maintain a cash reserve for unexpected expenses. Property renovations, market downturns, or tenant vacancies can strain your resources. Being financially prepared ensures you can weather the inevitable challenges that come with investing in transitioning neighborhoods.

Let's also consider the community impact. Investing in emerging neighborhoods isn't just about profits; it's about contributing to community growth. When done responsibly, your investment can enhance the quality of life for residents, increase housing options, and stimulate economic activity. Ethical investments aimed at improving community value create a sustainable, profitable environment for everyone.

In summary, mastering the art of investing in emerging neighborhoods involves a blend of rigorous research, strategic risk-taking, and a comprehensive understanding of market dynamics. It's about recognizing the silent signals and unseen opportunities, often hidden in plain sight. This proactive approach can transform your investment portfolio, setting you on the path toward substantial and sustainable wealth.

As we move forward in this book, we'll delve deeper into specific strategies, tools, and methodologies to help you identify and capitalize on these high-potential areas. From evaluating market conditions to leveraging technological tools, we'll arm you with the knowledge and tactics needed to confidently navigate the nuanced landscape of emerging neighborhood investments.

The journey to building wealth through real estate investment in emerging neighborhoods is both challenging and rewarding. It's a venture that requires patience, intelligence, and a commitment to lifelong learning. If you're willing to put in the effort, the results can lead to financial independence and a lasting legacy.

Section 1

Here, we'll discuss the foundational concepts underpinning investment in emerging neighborhoods.

- The transformative power of urban development
- Principles of identifying growth drivers
- Understanding community engagement initiatives

Investing in emerging neighborhoods is more than just a smart financial move—it's a journey of transformation, both for your financial future and the communities you invest in. So, let's get started on mastering this art, building your wealth, and making a meaningful impact along the way.

Chapter 2:
The Investment Landscape of
Emerging Neighborhoods

To thrive in the dynamic world of real estate, understanding the investment landscape of emerging neighborhoods is crucial. These areas often present compelling opportunities due to their untapped potential and lower entry barriers. As investors, it's essential to identify which neighborhoods are on the cusp of transformation by analyzing factors such as infrastructure development, economic incentives, and demographic trends. These elements serve as indicators of future growth and profitability. Diving into emerging markets requires a mix of meticulous research, strategic foresight, and a willingness to adapt to changing conditions. By recognizing the key drivers and basics of these burgeoning areas, you can position yourself to capitalise on significant returns, turning once-overlooked neighborhoods into pillars of your portfolio.

Understanding the Basics

At its core, investing in emerging neighborhoods is about recognizing potential before it becomes evident to the broader market. It requires a blend of market insight, local knowledge, and a keen eye for trends. This begs the question: what exactly constitutes an "emerging neighborhood"? In essence, it's an area on the cusp of significant growth and development, often characterized by rising property values, increasing commercial activity, and demographic shifts. These neighborhoods

9

may be transitioning from industrial to residential or experiencing an influx of new businesses and amenities.

One of the first steps in understanding these areas is recognizing the signs of emerging potential. Investors need to be aware of physical indicators such as new infrastructural projects or renovations. For instance, the presence of cranes, construction sites, and new businesses can signify impending growth. Moreover, demographic changes, such as an influx of younger professionals or artists, often hint at future development.

Understanding the fundamental economics at play is crucial. Property values in emerging neighborhoods typically start lower than those in established areas, which provides a lower entry price for investors. Over time, if the neighborhood develops as anticipated, the returns on investment can be substantial. It's essential to grasp this foundation to recognize why emerging neighborhoods can be such lucrative opportunities.

Another critical aspect is comprehending the role of local government and policies. Often, municipal support in the form of improved infrastructure, tax incentives, and rezoning initiatives acts as catalysts for neighborhood growth. Being knowledgeable about local government's plans can give investors an edge. For instance, a city might announce a significant revitalization project in a previously neglected district, signaling potential for future growth.

Investors should also familiarize themselves with the socio-economic fabric of these neighborhoods. Gentrification, while a contentious topic, is a common phenomenon in emerging areas. Understanding both the benefits and drawbacks of gentrification is vital. On one hand, it can increase property values and attract new businesses. On the other, it may displace long-standing residents, creating social and ethical considerations for investors.

In-depth market research is non-negotiable. Effective market analysis encompasses studying current property values, rental rates, vacancy rates, and sales trends. Using data-driven tools and resources can provide invaluable insights. Technology plays a significant role here, offering sophisticated analytics and market forecasting tools that were previously unavailable to individual investors.

It's also important to understand the role of commercial real estate in these neighborhoods. Often, the introduction of retail spaces, restaurants, and office buildings is an initial sign of an area's evolution. Commercial investments can sometimes yield higher returns compared to residential properties due to longer lease terms and stable tenants. Observing the type and pace of commercial development can offer clues about where the neighborhood is heading.

Risk management cannot be overlooked. Emerging neighborhoods come with inherent risks, including market volatility and the uncertainty of developmental timelines. Deploying effective risk management strategies, such as diversification and due diligence, can mitigate potential downsides. Investors should adopt a balanced approach, assessing both short-term gains and long-term growth prospects.

Understanding the timing is crucial. Entering an emerging market too early can mean a long wait for returns, while entering too late might mean heightened competition and reduced margins. The key is striking a balance—investing early enough to capitalize on growth, but with enough market indicators to justify the investment.

Investors need to stay informed about broader economic factors influencing these neighborhoods. Macroeconomic indicators such as interest rates, employment rates, and overall economic growth can impact real estate markets in emerging areas. Keeping an eye on these factors can provide context and assist with making informed decisions.

Networking with local stakeholders offers another layer of insight. Engaging with community leaders, real estate professionals, and even local residents can provide a ground-level view of neighborhood dynamics. These interactions can uncover opportunities and challenges that might not be evident through data analysis alone.

Finally, having a clear investment strategy is imperative. Emerging neighborhoods require a tailored approach, as the traditional rules of investing don't always apply. Setting specific goals, such as desired return on investment or property turnover rates, can guide your decision-making process.

In conclusion, understanding the basics of investing in emerging neighborhoods involves a multi-faceted approach. It's about combining data-driven analysis with local insights, balancing opportunities with risks, and having a strategic yet flexible investment plan. With the right foundation, investors can navigate the complexities of these dynamic markets and capitalize on untapped opportunities.

Identifying the Key Drivers of Growth

When it comes to identifying the key drivers of growth in emerging neighborhoods, you'll discover it's not just one singular factor but a confluence of various elements. These drivers can significantly influence investment decisions, turning a once overlooked area into a thriving hub of activity and profitability. Understanding these key drivers is essential for any investor looking to maximize their returns in emerging markets.

First, let's talk about *economic development*. One of the most powerful catalysts for growth in any neighborhood is economic opportunity. When new businesses move in, job opportunities increase. This influx can boost local incomes, property values, and overall economic health. Investors should keep an eye out for municipalities that are actively promoting economic development through tax incentives, grants, or other financial incentives aimed at attracting businesses.

Another critical driver is *demographic shifts*. Understanding who is moving into or out of a neighborhood can offer great insight into its future growth. Young professionals, for instance, often flock to areas with a vibrant cultural scene and strong employment prospects. Retirees may be attracted to regions with good healthcare and lower costs of living. Families might prioritize school quality and safety. By recognizing these demographic trends, investors can tailor their strategies to meet the specific needs and preferences of different population segments.

In addition to demographic shifts, *infrastructure development* often serves as a bellwether for growth. Projects such as new highways, public transit systems, or even the development of green spaces and recreational areas can dramatically enhance a neighborhood's appeal. These infrastructure enhancements can result in better accessibility and increased desirability, which ultimately drives up property values.

Educational institutions also play an instrumental role in shaping the dynamics of a neighborhood. Proximity to highly regarded colleges or universities can be a substantial pull factor, drawing students, academics, and staff, thereby creating demand for housing, retail, and entertainment facilities. This effect is often referred to as the "university effect" and can transform an ordinary neighborhood into a bustling epicenter of activity.

We can't overlook the pivotal role that *safety* and crime rates play in an investor's decision-making process. Areas that have successfully reduced crime and enhanced public safety see a correspondingly higher interest from potential residents and businesses. Police and community initiatives to curb crime can significantly impact the perception of a neighborhood, making it more attractive to new buyers and investors alike.

Another rising factor in modern neighborhood development is *technological integration*. Smart city initiatives, high-speed internet access, and other tech-driven amenities have started to become critical determinants in a neighborhood's growth potential. As remote work and digital lifestyles continue to proliferate, areas that offer advanced technological infrastructure gain a competitive edge.

Healthcare accessibility is another driver that should not be underestimated. Neighborhoods with proximity to top-tier healthcare facilities or specialized medical services appeal to a broader range of demographics. Whether for elderly residents, families, or young professionals, easy access to healthcare services is a critical consideration.

Let's not forget the *cultural and recreational amenities* that can transform a neighborhood's attractiveness. The presence of parks, theaters, museums, and dining establishments can significantly enhance the community's quality of life. These amenities serve as focal points for social gathering and community engagement, which are critical in making a neighborhood vibrant and appealing.

Environmental factors are also becoming increasingly important. Proximity to natural landscapes, water bodies, or even well-maintained green spaces can play a significant role in a neighborhood's growth. As urban dwellers seek more balanced lifestyles, areas that offer a mix of urban convenience and natural beauty are gaining prominence.

Investors should also take note of *market conditions* such as supply and demand dynamics, vacancy rates, and rental yields. High demand with low supply can drive property prices up, creating lucrative opportunities for investors. Monitoring these metrics can provide invaluable insights into the investment potential of emerging neighborhoods.

A sometimes overlooked but highly significant driver is *community engagement*. Areas with active and engaged communities often have higher levels of social cohesion, better local governance, and improved public services. These intangible elements can substantially contribute to the overall desirability and sustainability of a neighborhood's growth.

Lastly, one can't discount the importance of *government policies*. Zoning laws, tax incentives, and grants can either stifle or stimulate growth. Keeping abreast of local government initiatives and long-term planning can provide a strategic advantage when identifying potential investment opportunities.

In conclusion, identifying the key drivers of growth in emerging neighborhoods involves a comprehensive understanding of multiple intersecting factors. From economic development and demographic trends to infrastructure improvements and technological advancements, these elements collectively contribute to a neighborhood's potential for growth. For investors, having a keen eye on these drivers can transform potential risks into substantial rewards.

By closely monitoring these factors and adapting strategies accordingly, investors can position themselves to capitalize on the burgeoning opportunities present in emerging neighborhoods. Armed with this knowledge, you're better equipped to make informed decisions and achieve long-term success in the dynamic field of real estate investment.

Chapter 3:
The Economics of Emerging Markets

Understanding the economics of emerging markets is crucial for anyone looking to capitalize on untapped real estate opportunities. As these markets evolve, they often undergo significant economic transformations driven by factors such as urbanization, increased consumer spending, and foreign investments. Grasping the supply and demand dynamics, as well as evaluating current market conditions, can provide deep insights into future growth potential. Emerging markets often present a unique blend of volatility and opportunity, offering high returns for those who are willing to dive deep into market analysis and make informed decisions. For investors, entrepreneurs, and academics alike, harnessing the power of these economic trends can be the key to long-term wealth building and risk management in real estate ventures.

Evaluating Market Conditions

In the journey of understanding emerging markets, evaluating market conditions becomes a pivotal stage. It's the point where informed decisions are made, pivoting from mere speculation to strategic action. It's crucial to not just scratch the surface but delve deep into the indicators and markers that reveal a market's potential.

First off, let's revisit the very essence of what market conditions are. They encompass a wide array of factors, including but not limited to economic health, consumer confidence, employment rates, interest rates, and governmental policies. These components collectively paint a picture of the market's equilibrium at any given time. For investors, the objective is to interpret this canvas accurately.

Consider employment rates. High employment rates generally indicate a robust economy, translating into higher purchasing power for the population. This could mean an upsurge in demand for housing and commercial spaces, pushing property values upward. Conversely, areas experiencing high unemployment might indicate caution, suggesting a deeper look into local industries and potential recovery plans before investing.

Interest rates are another critical aspect. Lower interest rates often make borrowing cheaper, facilitating an increase in property purchases and developments. As rates rise, borrowing becomes more expensive, usually leading to a dip in real estate activities. Understanding how current and projected interest rates align with your investment horizon helps in timing your entries and exits more effectively.

Moreover, evaluating consumer confidence can offer a window into future market behavior. Confidence indices signal how optimistic or pessimistic consumers are about their financial health and the general state of the economy. High consumer confidence generally correlates with higher spending, and that includes buying homes and investing in properties. If the consumer sentiment is in the dumps, you might want to tread carefully.

Don't overlook the importance of demographic trends. Pay attention to shifts such as population growth, age distribution, and income levels. For instance, an influx of younger professionals into a neighborhood often leads to gentrification. These areas can see substantial real estate appreciation due to an increase in demand for modern amenities, trendy housing, and commercial activities. Recognizing these patterns early can spell the difference between a good investment and a great one.

Let's pivot to governmental regulations. How friendly or stringent is local legislation regarding real estate development? Are there new zoning laws or tax incentives that could affect property values? Local government policies can significantly impact investment conditions. Policies such as tax relief for new buyers or subsidies for commercial development can spur rapid growth, making certain markets especially attractive.

Economic indicators like Gross Domestic Product (GDP) growth rates should be on your radar too. A growing GDP generally indicates an expanding economy, which often results in higher real estate demand. Many emerging markets show impressive GDP growth rates, presenting tantalizing opportunities for the astute investor.

If considering international investment, be attentive to currency fluctuations. Exchange rate stability is crucial when investing abroad, as sudden changes can either unexpectedly boost your gains or erode your investment's value. Currency trends often correlate with the broader economic health of a country, and staying informed can save you from costly surprises.

Navigating market conditions also involves understanding the supply and demand dynamics, but that's a topic to delve into separately. For now, it's enough to grasp that indicators such as vacancy rates and new construction permits can offer invaluable insights into future supply trends and demand pressures.

Another increasingly important angle is the environmental sustainability of potential investments. With the global shift towards "green" building practices, locations emphasizing sustainable development can present long-term value. Properties in these areas often benefit from lower operating costs and increased attractiveness to eco-conscious tenants and buyers. Plus, some governments offer incentives for sustainable projects, enhancing potential returns.

While quantitative data forms the backbone of evaluating market conditions, qualitative insights shouldn't be underestimated. Often, conversations with local experts, real estate agents, city planners, and community leaders can offer a nuanced view that's not readily apparent in raw data. They can provide context to statistics and reveal undercurrents that might not yet be fully reflected in the numbers.

Another point of focus is the geopolitical climate. Political stability often correlates with economic stability, providing a more secure environment for investments. Conversely, regions rife with political turmoil or conflict can present heightened risks that might outweigh potential rewards.

To ensure thoroughness, always compare multiple sources of information. Relying on a single report or data set can lead to biased or incomplete conclusions. Use tools like market research software and property management platforms to gather, analyze, and cross-verify data. Technology has made it easier than ever to access real-time information, and leveraging these tools can provide a competitive edge.

Finally, remember that no market condition is static. Regularly review and reassess the market conditions to stay adaptive and responsive to changes. This flexibility can be the key to long-term success in real estate investing, especially in the dynamic landscapes of emerging markets. By honing the skill to evaluate and react to market conditions, you position yourself advantageously in the pursuit of strategic real estate investments.

Supply and Demand Dynamics

In the realm of emerging markets, understanding the intricacies of supply and demand dynamics is crucial for maximizing investment potential. Unlike more established markets, emerging regions often exhibit volatile supply and demand characteristics that can either pose risks or present extraordinary opportunities. Investors need to be adept at reading these signals to time their entry and exit strategies effectively.

One of the most compelling aspects of emerging markets is the pace at which demand can shift. These areas may attract new residents, businesses, and investors rapidly, leading to swift rises in property values. A sudden influx of a tech company, for example, can create a cascade of demand for housing and related services. This brisk demand can create a sense of urgency, pushing prices up and making early investments particularly lucrative.

Simultaneously, supply in these markets is often constrained initially. Zoning laws, land availability, and the time it takes to construct new buildings all contribute to a lag in supply meeting demand. In established areas, developers might hesitate to build speculatively due to more predictable and capped growth. However, in emerging markets, the potential for substantial gains encourages developers to act quickly, sometimes taking calculated risks to meet the surging demand.

Another interesting element to consider is the role of speculative investments. In established markets, speculation often leads to instability. However, in emerging markets, speculative investment can sometimes stimulate growth, driving up early demand and attracting more conservative investors later on. This domino effect can spur extensive development, turning fledgling neighborhoods into thriving communities.

Moreover, government policies play an influential role in shaping supply and demand. Local administrations in emerging markets might enact policies to encourage growth, from tax incentives to relaxed zoning laws. Such measures can significantly impact both supply and demand. By making it easier and more profitable to develop properties, these policies can lead to an uptick in supply, attempting to balance the burgeoning demand but often creating a cyclical effect that fuels further growth.

On the flip side, high demand without corresponding supply can lead to a different set of challenges. Property prices may inflate rapidly, making it difficult for average buyers to enter the market. This can shift the investor landscape towards high-net-worth individuals and institutional investors, thereby altering the dynamics of the market. The law of diminishing returns starts to come into play, and without new supply, the market may face a bubble risk.

It's also essential to recognize the role of demographic shifts in influencing demand. Areas with growing populations, particularly younger demographics looking for affordable housing, typically see sustained demand. Emerging markets often appeal to younger citizens due to lower cost of living and potential job growth. These demographic factors must be taken into account when analyzing supply and demand.

Conversely, if an emerging market sees a decline in population or interest due to economic or social factors, the demand might plummet, leaving a glut of properties. Savvy investors should keep an eye on demographic trends and be prepared to pivot their strategies accordingly. It's not just about the current state of demand but anticipating how it will evolve over time.

The economic health of the area also plays a significant role. Areas that are experiencing job growth, rising incomes, and investment in infrastructure are likely to see a more stable balance of supply and demand. The ripple effect of economic prosperity can lead to sustained demand, encouraging more developers to supply the market with new projects.

Another aspect to consider is the nature of demand itself. Emerging markets often showcase diverse forms of demand, from residential to commercial and even industrial. Each type of demand can impact the other. For instance, a rise in residential demand might spur commercial development as businesses move in to cater to the increasing population. This interconnectedness is a hallmark of emerging markets and something keen investors can leverage.

Investors should also be aware of global factors influencing local markets. Economic shifts in leading global markets, changes in foreign investment policies, and even geopolitical stability can impact supply and demand dynamics in emerging markets. A rise in foreign interest can spike demand and drive up prices, while global economic downturns might lead to reduced investments and a surplus in supply.

Understanding the supply chain aspects of construction can also be critical. In emerging markets, the ability to swiftly mobilize construction efforts depends on available resources, workforce, and regulatory environment. Interruptions in this supply chain, such as material shortages or workforce challenges, can delay projects and impact the equilibrium of supply and demand.

Additionally, environmental factors can play unforeseen roles in shaping supply and demand. Natural disasters, climate change impacts, and other environmental conditions can affect the desirability and availability of real estate in emerging markets. Areas prone to flooding or other natural disasters might see a fluctuating demand pattern that investors need to monitor and mitigate.

In conclusion, the supply and demand dynamics in emerging markets are both a challenge and an opportunity. By understanding and anticipating how these forces interact, investors can make strategic decisions that not only capitalize on immediate gains but also foster long-term growth. The key lies in continuous market analysis, staying informed about local and global trends, monitoring demographic shifts, and always being prepared to adapt to changing conditions. Successful navigation of these dynamics can turn emerging markets into the cornerstone of a diversified and profitable real estate investment portfolio.

Chapter 4:
Opportunities in Residential Properties

Residential properties remain a cornerstone of real estate investment, offering a plethora of opportunities for wealth-building through both single-family homes and multi-family units. With a growing demand for housing driven by population growth and urbanization, investors can capitalize on these dynamics by strategically identifying areas poised for appreciation and rental income. Single-family homes provide stability and a steady cash flow, making them ideal for investors seeking lower risk. On the other hand, multi-family units not only offer higher returns but also the advantage of economies of scale, which can significantly boost profitability. By leveraging market analysis, understanding local demographics, and keeping an eye on infrastructure developments, investors can navigate the residential property landscape effectively, turning potential challenges into lucrative opportunities. The real key lies in thorough due diligence and a long-term vision, positioning oneself to tap into growth and secure lasting financial gains.

Single-Family Homes

When we talk about opportunities in residential properties, single-family homes hold a unique charm. They're often the first investment choice for new real estate investors, and for good reason. These properties offer a blend of stability and appreciation potential, making them a reliable entry point into the world of real estate. But don't mistake their simplicity for a lack of opportunity. The key is knowing where to look and what to evaluate when considering single-family homes as an investment.

Single-family homes typically appeal to a wide range of potential buyers and renters, from young families to retirees. The consistent demand across diverse demographic groups adds a layer of security to your investment. Moreover, these properties are relatively straightforward to manage and finance. Lenders are often more flexible with financing single-family homes compared to multi-family units or commercial properties, which can make this avenue more accessible for new investors.

One of the prime advantages of single-family homes is their flexibility. Whether you plan to flip the property, rent it out, or hold it for long-term appreciation, there are multiple strategies you can employ. The market for single-family homes in emerging neighborhoods is ripe with potential. As these areas develop, the value of properties tends to appreciate faster than in more established neighborhoods.

Understanding market dynamics is crucial. Start with a comprehensive market analysis. Look for emerging neighborhoods where job growth, infrastructure development, and demographic shifts point to an upward trend in property values. Identifying these trends early can position you to capitalize on significant appreciation.

Investing in single-family homes requires due diligence. Evaluate the property's condition, the quality of local schools, crime rates, and access to amenities. Each of these factors contributes to the property's desirability and potential for appreciation. Access to good schools, in particular, can be a significant draw for families, ensuring a stable tenant pool or a quick resale if you choose to flip the property.

Renovations and Upgrades

In many cases, single-family homes in emerging neighborhoods might need some updating or renovations. This creates an opportunity for value-add investment strategies. Simple upgrades like modern kitchens, updated bathrooms, and improved landscaping can significantly increase a property's market value. Be cautious not to over-improve; the goal is to match the property's quality with neighborhood standards to ensure you don't price yourself out of the market.

Smart renovations with a focus on energy efficiency and sustainability can also attract eco-conscious renters or buyers willing to pay a premium. Features like solar panels, energy-efficient windows, and sustainable landscaping not only boost property value but also reduce ongoing costs for tenants, making the property even more attractive.

Cash Flow and Rental Yields

For those interested in rental income, single-family homes offer good cash flow potential. The key is in the property location and purchase price. Aim to buy at a price that allows you to cover mortgage payments, property taxes, insurance, and maintenance costs while still generating a positive cash flow. Consider using tools and calculators that can help forecast rental income and expenses to ensure the property meets your investment criteria.

Emerging neighborhoods often have lower purchase costs but can achieve competitive rental rates, providing better yields than established, higher-cost areas. Additionally, single-family homes tend to have lower vacancy rates compared to multi-family units as they attract long-term tenants who value the stability and comfort of a home.

Tenant management is another aspect of investing in single-family homes. While managing tenants can be time-consuming, it's often less complex than managing larger multi-family units with a higher tenant turnover rate. Effective tenant screening and robust lease agreements can mitigate many potential issues and ensure a steady, reliable rental income.

Leveraging Financing Options

Financing single-family homes can be more straightforward than other property types. Conventional loans, FHA loans, and even VA loans offer accessible financing options with varying down payment requirements and interest rates. The relative ease of securing financing makes single-family homes an attractive option for investors who might not have substantial capital on hand but are willing to tap into mortgage options.

Another financing strategy is to leverage equity from existing properties. If you own a home or have other real estate assets with built-up equity, consider using a home equity line of credit (HELOC) to fund new investments. This method allows you to capitalize on your current assets while expanding your portfolio.

Risks and Mitigation Strategies

It's important to recognize the risks associated with single-family home investments. Market fluctuations, unexpected repairs, and tenant issues can all impact your bottom line. However, these risks can be managed. Diversifying your investment portfolio, maintaining a fund for unexpected expenses, and thorough market research can mitigate many of these risks.

Your investing strategy should include a clear exit strategy. Whether you plan to hold the property long-term, flip it after improvements, or convert it into a rental, having a defined exit plan can ensure you stay focused on your investment goals and make informed decisions.

In conclusion, single-family homes offer a compelling entry point into real estate investment with multiple opportunities for profit and growth. By conducting thorough market research, managing risks thoughtfully, and leveraging strategic financing, you can unlock significant value and set yourself on a path to long-term wealth through real estate. Remember, the journey doesn't end with the first purchase—

it's just the beginning of building a robust and diversified real estate portfolio.

Multi-Family Units

When it comes to opportunities in residential properties, multi-family units stand out as a particularly promising investment. Unlike single-family homes, multi-family properties — such as duplexes, triplexes, and apartment complexes — offer a distinct set of advantages that can significantly enhance both short-term cash flow and long-term wealth accumulation. This section dives into why these properties should capture the attention of both novice and seasoned investors.

Let's start with the basics: multi-family units inherently offer multiple revenue streams. With several rental units within a single property, the risk of vacancy is diversified. Even if one unit is vacant, the income from the other units can still cover a significant portion of the operating expenses and the mortgage. In contrast, a single-family home offers only one income stream, leaving the investor fully exposed to vacancy risks. This makes multi-family properties an attractive and less risky option for income-driven investors.

Moreover, multi-family units often generate higher returns per square foot compared to single-family homes. This is largely because of economies of scale. For instance, property management fees, maintenance costs, and utilities can be more efficiently managed and spread across multiple units, lowering the per-unit cost. The potential for higher net operating income (NOI) makes multi-family properties particularly appealing for those looking to maximize their investment returns.

Financing these kinds of properties can also provide unique opportunities. Lenders often view multi-family units as lower-risk investments, particularly if the property has a strong occupancy rate and is located in a growing neighborhood. As a result, investors may find it easier to secure favorable loan terms. Additionally, government-backed loans, such as those from the Federal Housing Administration (FHA), may offer beneficial terms specifically for multi-unit properties, making it easier to enter the multi-unit investment space.

An essential consideration when investing in multi-family properties is market demand. Urbanization trends, demographic shifts, and lifestyle changes are driving increased demand for rental housing, especially in emerging neighborhoods. Young professionals, downsizing baby boomers, and those seeking more affordable housing options are all contributing to this rising demand. Keeping a finger on the pulse of these trends can help investors make well-informed decisions about where and when to invest in multi-family units.

Location is always critical in real estate, but it takes on added importance for multi-family units. Proximity to employment centers, educational institutions, transportation hubs, and amenities significantly influences the desirability of a rental property. It's vital to perform thorough due diligence to identify neighborhoods that are poised for growth and can attract long-term tenants. This involves not just current market data but also forward-looking assessments of infrastructure development, zoning changes, and demographic shifts.

Arguably, one of the most compelling advantages of multi-family investments is their scalability. As your investment portfolio grows, managing a larger number of single-family homes can become increasingly complex and time-consuming. Conversely, scaling up with multi-family units can be more streamlined. For instance, managing a 50-unit apartment complex often involves less logistical hassle than managing 50 individual homes across different locations. This scalability can make a significant difference in the efficiency and profitability of a real estate portfolio.

Managing multi-family properties does come with its challenges. High tenant turnover, maintenance of common areas, and coordinating lease agreements require a more hands-on approach than single-family homes. However, professional property management services can alleviate these burdens, allowing investors to focus on growth strategies rather than day-to-day operations. Though these services come with a cost, the benefits usually far outweigh the expenses, particularly in larger multi-family properties.

It's also crucial to understand the legal and regulatory landscape that governs multi-family units. These properties are subject to more stringent building codes, safety regulations, and tenant rights laws. Understanding these regulations and ensuring compliance is essential to avoid potential legal pitfalls. Many jurisdictions also offer incentives for building or renovating multi-family units, particularly if they include affordable housing options. These incentives can further boost the returns on investment and mitigate risks.

One should not overlook the social impact of multi-family investments. By providing housing solutions in emerging neighborhoods, investors can contribute to community revitalization and economic development. Ethically managed properties can enhance the quality of life for tenants, offering well-maintained living spaces, fostering community, and supporting local businesses. This dual opportunity for financial gain and positive social impact can be especially motivating for investors who seek to make a difference with their investment choices.

In summary, multi-family units offer a multifaceted approach to real estate investing that combines the potential for robust income, scalability, and risk diversification. By understanding the unique benefits and challenges of these properties, investors can make strategic decisions that align with their financial goals and broader market trends. Emerging neighborhoods, with their growth potential and evolving demographics, provide a fertile ground for these investments. Harnessing the power of multi-family units can be a cornerstone strategy for building a resilient, profitable real estate portfolio.

Chapter 5:
Commercial Real Estate:
A Hidden Gem

Commercial real estate, often overshadowed by its residential counterpart, presents an untapped reservoir of potential for both seasoned and budding investors. Unlike residential properties, which can be more susceptible to market volatility, commercial assets like retail spaces and office buildings often benefit from stable, long-term leases, providing consistent cash flow. This sector is an intricate blend of opportunity and complexity, requiring keen market insights and strategic vision. Investors who diversify into commercial real estate can leverage its unique advantages—economic resilience, tenant diversity, and significant growth potential. By tapping into this hidden gem, you're not just adding another asset to your portfolio; you're forging a path toward robust, sustainable investment returns. The challenges are real, but so are the rewards for those willing to navigate the nuanced world of commercial property investment.

Retail Spaces

Commercial real estate represents a vast and often underexplored domain for those looking to make profitable investments. Within this sector, retail spaces stand out as a particularly viable and dynamic area. Retail real estate encompasses a variety of property types, including storefronts, shopping malls, strip centers, and even pop-up shops in prime locations. Investors aiming to tap into this segment need to understand the unique opportunities and challenges it presents.

One of the greatest advantages of investing in retail spaces is the potential for high returns. Unlike residential properties, which usually offer predictable but restrained revenue, retail spaces can generate substantial income, particularly if the property is located in a thriving area. A well-chosen retail property can yield rental incomes that significantly exceed those of similar-sized residential investments. The key is to identify areas with high foot traffic and evolving consumer trends.

Understanding consumer behavior is crucial for retail investments. The success of retail spaces heavily relies on the right mix of tenants. Merchants that complement each other and draw a steady stream of foot traffic will create a symbiotic environment where all tenants thrive. This upstream effect results in lower vacancy rates and, consequently, more consistent rental income. Therefore, investors must be adept at evaluating tenant potential and understanding market needs.

Location is another vital aspect of retail real estate investment. Properties situated in areas experiencing economic growth, infrastructural development, and demographic shifts often offer significant investment potential. Gentrifying neighborhoods, for example, can provide lucrative opportunities to acquire retail spaces at more affordable prices before property values soar. Urban planners and market researchers can be invaluable allies in pinpointing these budding hotspots.

Investors also need to be mindful of the evolving nature of retail. The rise of e-commerce challenged traditional brick-and-mortar stores and led many to believe that physical retail spaces would become obsolete. However, the current trend shows that retail spaces are far from dying out but are rather evolving. The synergy between online and offline sales, known as omnichannel retail, has become increasingly important. Retailers now leverage physical spaces to enhance customer experience, offer click-and-collect options, and provide in-store events.

Investors who recognize and adapt to these shifts can turn what others see as a challenge into an opportunity.

Furthermore, retail spaces can offer diverse investment options. High-street retail properties in busy downtown areas might require a larger capital outlay but offer the benefit of stable, high-quality tenants. On the other hand, neighborhood shopping centers or strip malls, though less glamorous, can achieve high yields if they cater to the daily needs of the community. These properties often house essential services like grocery stores, pharmacies, and personal care shops, which tend to have a stable demand regardless of economic fluctuations.

One must also consider the role of niche markets within retail spaces. For example, specialty retail centers focusing on a particular sector, such as technology, fashion, or wellness, can capture the attention of target demographics effectively. Pop-up retail, where temporary stores are established to capitalize on high-demand seasons or events, is another model gaining traction. Investors can benefit from the flexibility and lower upfront costs associated with pop-up shops while still earning substantial short-term returns.

In addition, mixed-use developments incorporating retail spaces can offer excellent investment prospects. These complexes integrate residential, office, and retail space into a single property, creating a built-in customer base for the retail tenants. Such synergies can enhance property values and reduce risks by diversifying income streams. Urban planning trends increasingly favor mixed-use developments for their efficiency and potential to create vibrant, walkable communities.

It's also essential for investors to grasp the regulatory environment impacting retail spaces. Zoning laws, property taxes, and various permits can all influence the viability of a retail investment. Navigating these regulations requires due diligence, but it also presents opportunities—areas with favorable tax incentives, for instance, can significantly improve the profitability of a retail property.

Risk management remains a critical component of any retail real estate investment strategy. Diversifying across different types of retail properties and geographical locations can help mitigate risks. Legal considerations, such as securing long-term leases with escalation clauses that adjust for inflation, are vital to ensure stable income streams. Engaging with experienced property managers can also minimize operational risks, ensuring that properties remain well-maintained and attract desirable tenants.

Innovative technology can streamline the process of investing in and managing retail spaces. Tools for market research can help identify promising locations and tenant mix, while property management software can assist in handling maintenance requests, lease agreements, and rent collection. Leveraging technology can make the difference between a good investment and a great one.

Lastly, retail spaces offer investors the chance to engage in socially responsible investing. Supporting local businesses, enhancing community spaces, and participating in sustainable developments can provide not only financial returns but also social and environmental benefits. Investors who prioritize these aspects often find themselves more integrated within the community, leading to more robust, long-term investment prospects.

In conclusion, retail spaces in commercial real estate offer a hidden gem of opportunity for discerning investors. From understanding consumer behavior to leveraging location benefits and embracing new retail trends, there are numerous ways to maximize returns in this vibrant sector. Investors willing to conduct thorough research, manage risks effectively, and adapt to changing market conditions will find retail spaces to be a rewarding addition to their investment portfolios.

Office Buildings

Office buildings are a cornerstone of the commercial real estate sector. They offer a diversity of opportunities for investors seeking stable, long-term returns. These structures, spanning everything from high-rises in urban centers to suburban office parks, can be a reliable investment if approached strategically.

The location of an office building plays a crucial role in its potential profitability. Urban centers often attract businesses due to their access to amenities and talent pools. On the other hand, suburban office buildings can appeal to companies looking for more space at a lower cost. The right location can significantly impact vacancy rates and rental income.

Modern office buildings are evolving. Open-floor plans, flexible workspaces, and technology integration are now standard features. These attractions cater to contemporary businesses that prioritize employee wellness, collaboration, and efficiency. Investors should look for buildings that can easily adapt to new design trends and technological advancements.

One key factor to consider when investing in office buildings is the lease structure. Long-term leases with reputable tenants can provide a predictable income stream. Conversely, shorter lease terms might allow for quicker adjustments in rent, responding to market conditions.

Before diving into an office building investment, it's vital to perform thorough due diligence. Assess the property's current occupancy rates, the creditworthiness of existing tenants, and the potential for future rent increases. Understanding the dynamics of the local office market—such as demand trends and new supply—can offer a competitive edge.

Particularly for higher-end office spaces, sustainability and energy efficiency are growing priorities. Leadership in Energy and Environmental Design (LEED) certification can be a significant draw for tenants who value environmentally friendly practices. Such certifications can also reduce operating costs, benefiting the bottom line.

Cap rates, or capitalization rates, are another critical metric for evaluating office buildings. They help investors understand the potential return relative to the property's purchase price. A higher cap rate might indicate more risk, while a lower cap rate often suggests a property in a prime location with stable income.

Investors shouldn't overlook the importance of amenities and services. On-site cafeterias, fitness centers, and even childcare facilities can differentiate one office building from another. Buildings that offer robust amenities are more likely to attract and retain desirable tenants.

The rise of remote work and coworking spaces introduces both opportunities and challenges. While remote work might reduce demand for traditional office space, it also fosters the growth of flexible office arrangements. Investing in properties that can accommodate such flexibility can be a smart move.

Office buildings in emerging neighborhoods present unique opportunities. These areas might not yet have sky-high property prices but show significant signs of growth. Investing in such locales can capitalize on early-stage development and appreciation.

Maintenance and management play crucial roles in the success of office building investments. Keeping the property in top condition ensures tenant satisfaction and reduces turnover. Third-party property management companies can streamline these processes, allowing investors to focus on strategic decisions.

The economic cycle can influence office building investments. During economic upswings, demand for office space typically increases, driving up rents and occupancy rates. Conversely, economic downturns can lead to higher vacancies. Diversification can help mitigate these risks.

Technological advancements can enhance the operational efficiency of office buildings. Smart building technologies, such as automated lighting, heating, and security systems, can reduce operating costs and improve tenant satisfaction. Staying ahead of such trends can make an investment more lucrative.

It's crucial to understand the competitive landscape when considering an office building investment. What other developments are in the pipeline? How does the property compare with nearby alternatives? A SWOT analysis—assessing strengths, weaknesses, opportunities, and threats—can provide valuable insights.

One often overlooked aspect is the potential for mixed-use developments. Combining office space with retail or residential units can diversify income streams and enhance property value. Urban planners and developers increasingly favor such integrated approaches.

Negotiating favorable terms with service providers, like janitorial or security services, can also positively impact the bottom line. These service contracts play a significant role in the overall operating expenses of a property.

Understanding regulatory frameworks and zoning laws is essential for office building investments. Some locations might offer tax incentives for developing or refurbishing office spaces. Being aware of these can add an extra layer of profitability to an investment.

Finally, market research is indispensable. Use reliable market research tools to analyze trends, gather data, and make informed decisions. Leveraging technology for market analysis can set you apart from less prepared investors. By staying informed, you can better anticipate market shifts and adapt your strategy accordingly.

The potential of office buildings in the commercial real estate sector is vast. With strategic planning, thorough due diligence, and staying abreast of emerging trends, these investments can yield substantial returns. Whether you're an experienced investor or new to the field, the office building sector offers numerous pathways to financial growth and long-term success.

In summary, office buildings are more than just bricks and mortar; they are dynamic investments influenced by location, market conditions, and evolving workplace trends. By focusing on adaptability, amenities, and market research, investors can unlock significant value in this promising sector.

Chapter 6:
Analyzing Neighborhood Potential

Understanding the potential of a neighborhood is crucial for making strategic real estate investments. Investors must pay close attention to demographic shifts and infrastructure development, as these factors play a significant role in determining a neighborhood's future value. Look beyond current property prices and investigate trends in population growth, age distribution, and income levels. Also, consider planned and ongoing infrastructure projects like new schools, hospitals, and transportation hubs, as these can greatly enhance the desirability of an area. By combining thorough market research with an eye for detail, you can identify neighborhoods on the verge of transformation, enabling you to make informed decisions that maximize returns and support long-term wealth creation.

Demographic Shifts

At the heart of understanding any neighborhood's potential lies the analysis of demographic shifts. These shifts, often taking years to unfold, can transform an area from a sleepy backwater into a bustling hub of activity. Recognizing these transformations in their early stages can offer unparalleled opportunities for astute investors. So, let's dive into why these changes matter and how you can harness them for maximum benefit.

The most apparent demographic shift often revolves around age groups. For example, an influx of younger families can signal a burgeoning market for schools, daycare centers, and family-oriented retail stores. Conversely, an increase in elderly residents might prompt demand for healthcare services, assisted living facilities, and leisure activities tailored for older adults. Identifying these patterns can guide your investment focus, allowing you to target properties and businesses that will meet emerging needs.

Ethnic and Cultural Changes

Ethnic and cultural shifts are equally impactful. Newcomers from different cultural backgrounds bring with them distinct lifestyles, food preferences, and community habits. Areas experiencing an influx of a specific ethnic group can see a rise in ethnic restaurants, specialty stores, and cultural centers. By recognizing these trends early, investors can tap into niche markets that can offer excellent returns.

For example, think about the explosion of Little Italy-like neighborhoods in various American cities. These enclaves didn't just happen overnight; they were nurtured over years of demographic change, attracting people with similar cultural backgrounds, followed by businesses that catered to their needs. Similarly, Hispanic populations moving into a neighborhood can bolster local economies through the creation of authentic culinary experiences and retail spaces.

Shifting Income Levels

Income shifts are another critical factor. As residents' incomes rise, so does their spending capacity. This can transform a previously modest neighborhood into an upscale area teeming with high-end retailers, gourmet dining, and luxury housing. The reverse is also true; a decline in income levels can prompt a need for affordable housing and budget-friendly services. Keeping an eye on income trends can help you predict the kind of investments that will be profitable.

Also, understand that income shifts often go hand-in-hand with educational and occupational changes. New, more affluent residents might be drawn to an area due to improved school ratings or the establishment of corporate offices nearby. Consequently, the real estate market can see a shift from rental properties to owned homes, transforming the neighborhood's investment profile.

Population Growth: The Real Game Changer

Population growth is the cornerstone of demographic shifts. An expanding population translates to increased demand for housing, retail spaces, and essential services. But it's not just the numbers that matter; the composition of that population growth is equally significant. Are these new residents young professionals, retirees, or families? The answer will guide your investment strategy markedly.

Areas experiencing population booms often see skyrocketing real estate values. Early investors who identify these growth spots can purchase properties at lower prices, enjoying substantial appreciation over just a few years. The trick lies in recognizing the signals of impending population growth, which often includes new businesses opening, infrastructural developments, and an influx of amenities.

A Dual Perspective: Micro and Macro Trends

Analyzing demographic shifts requires a dual approach: micro and macro perspectives. Macro-level analysis focuses on large-scale trends, like national and regional population shifts, while micro-level scrutiny hones in on local factors. Combining these perspectives ensures a comprehensive understanding of the neighborhood's trajectory.

For instance, macro trends might indicate a national movement toward urban living, prompting you to consider inner-city neighborhoods ripe for investment. However, a micro-level analysis could reveal that a specific urban area is seeing a decline due to poor school performance or high crime rates. Thus, balancing both perspectives provides a more accurate picture, helping you make informed, strategic decisions.

Leveraging Data and Technology

Tapping into technology and data analytics can dramatically enhance your ability to foresee demographic shifts. Various online tools and databases offer real-time demographic data, helping you monitor changes dynamically. Platforms like census databases and real estate analytic tools can furnish insights into age distribution, income levels, and even migration patterns. Utilizing these resources can offer a significant edge in making timely, informed investment decisions.

Consider investing in property analytics software which can offer real-time insights into demographic dynamics. These tools can alert you to shifts you might otherwise miss, predominantly if they're incremental. Technology, when aptly leveraged, transforms demographic analysis from a cumbersome chore into a streamlined process.

The Psychological Aspect

While data is invaluable, don't underestimate the importance of the psychological aspect. Often, demographic shifts are preceded by subtle societal changes. By keeping your ear to the ground—participating in community meetings, following local news, and even casual conversations—you can sense impending changes before they become evident in data reports. This qualitative insight often complements your quantitative analysis, providing a holistic view of neighborhood potential.

For example, an uptick in community activism or local government initiatives can signal a neighborhood on the brink of revitalization. Paying attention to such grassroots movements can offer foresight into which areas will likely undergo profitable transformations.

Challenges and Pitfalls

Like any other aspect of real estate investment, analyzing demographic shifts isn't without its challenges. For one, demographic data can sometimes be misleading. It's essential to cross-reference multiple data points to ensure accuracy. Additionally, demographic shifts can be slow to manifest in a way that directly impacts property values, requiring patience and long-term commitment.

Moreover, external factors like changes in immigration policies or economic downturns can abruptly alter demographic trends, throwing a wrench into even the best-laid plans. Thus, it's crucial to continually monitor and reassess your strategies, adapting to new information as it becomes available.

Success Stories: Proven Impact

To illustrate the transformative impact of demographic shifts, consider the success of various urban renewal projects. Neighborhoods like Brooklyn in New York or the Pearl District in Portland were once considered undesirable but have since become some of the most sought-after locales. These transformations were driven by a series of demographic shifts—young professionals moving in, followed by families, eventually attracting businesses catering to these groups.

Another example is the tech boom in cities like Austin and San Francisco. The influx of tech workers with higher disposable incomes has dramatically altered the urban landscape, pushing property values sky-high and creating a robust demand for both residential and commercial properties. Investors who recognized these shifts early have reaped substantial returns.

The Way Forward

Understanding demographic shifts is more than just crunching numbers; it's about understanding people and their evolving needs and preferences. By combining data analysis with qualitative insights and staying attuned to both micro and macro trends, you can unlock unparalleled opportunities.

So, as you chart your course through the complex waters of real estate investment, remember to keep a vigilant eye on demographic shifts. They're the keys that can unlock hidden treasures in

Infrastructure Development

The development of infrastructure stands as a cornerstone in evaluating the potential of an emerging neighborhood. For investors, understanding the various aspects of infrastructure—ranging from transportation networks to utility services—can be a game-changer. Infrastructure can make or break the growth trajectory of a neighborhood and, consequently, the returns on your investment.

First, let's talk about transportation networks. Well-developed transportation options—such as highways, public transit systems, and bike lanes—are critical factors that influence a neighborhood's appeal. The more accessible an area is, the more attractive it becomes to potential residents and businesses. Properties near major transportation hubs usually appreciate faster, as they offer convenience that adds tangible value. In your evaluations, pay close attention to projects like new subway lines, bus routes, or highway expansions. These can significantly enhance property values in the vicinity and should not be overlooked.

Beyond the movement of people, the availability and quality of utilities are also of prime importance. Stable electricity, high-speed internet, clean water, and efficient waste management systems are fundamental for both residential and commercial properties. An emerging neighborhood that's well-served by these utilities can attract tech companies, entrepreneurs, and remote workers who rely heavily on such services. Evaluating infrastructure goes beyond just checking what's available; it's about assessing the reliability and future upgrades of these services as well.

Healthcare facilities and educational institutions are often overlooked but represent critical pieces of a neighborhood's infrastructure. Proximity to good schools and hospitals can significantly impact property values. Families, in particular, prioritize these elements when deciding where to live. When assessing an emerging neighborhood, take note of existing schools and hospitals. Look for planned improvements or new facilities as indicators of growth.

In addition to these basic services, recreational and cultural infrastructure can play a huge role in elevating a neighborhood's status. Parks, theaters, museums, and sports facilities contribute to the livability and attractiveness of an area. Such amenities not only increase the quality of life for residents but also draw in tourists and boost local businesses, adding another layer of potential revenue streams for investors. A balanced blend of green spaces and cultural venues makes an area multidimensional, appealing to a broader demographic.

One of the less obvious but equally essential forms of infrastructure is technological readiness. In today's digital age, a neighborhood equipped with smart city features—such as Wi-Fi-enabled public spaces, smart traffic lights, or even efficient public surveillance systems—can make it more enticing for tech-savvy residents and businesses. Future-proofing your investments should involve a keen eye on how technology is being incorporated into the city's infrastructure plans.

Government initiatives and planned investments can serve as signals for budding infrastructure development. Public records, town hall meetings, and planning commission reports are gold mines of information. Governments often provide blueprints and timelines for upcoming infrastructure projects. Being ahead of the curve in recognizing these signals allows you to capitalize on growth before the rest of the market catches on. Be proactive in your approach to discover which areas are receiving attention and funding from municipal, state, or federal agencies.

Let's not forget about environmental infrastructure. Sustainable, eco-friendly initiatives like green roofing, rainwater harvesting, and renewable energy projects contribute to a neighborhood's appeal in today's environmentally-conscious world. These eco-friendly developments make properties attractive to a growing segment of green-conscious buyers and renters. Sustainability in infrastructure is more than a trend; it's becoming a standard expectation, increasing the intrinsic value of properties in these neighborhoods.

Furthermore, the symbiotic relationship between commercial and residential developments can't be overstressed. A balance between housing and commercial real estate ensures a self-sustaining neighborhood. Retail stores, office spaces, and entertainment venues should be easily accessible to residents. Mixed-use developments, where commercial and residential spaces co-exist, are becoming increasingly popular for this very reason. They create vibrant, dynamic neighborhoods where people can live, work, and play without long commutes.

Lastly, don't underestimate the power of community-based infrastructure projects. Community centers, libraries, and local markets create a sense of belonging and engagement among residents. These facilities often form the social backbone of a neighborhood, contributing to its stability and desirability. Popular community-driven events or local farmers' markets can serve as indicators of an active, engaged community, adding another layer of value to the neighborhood.

In conclusion, evaluating infrastructure development is a multifaceted endeavor requiring thorough research and a holistic perspective. From transportation and utility services to healthcare, education, recreation, technological readiness, and environmental initiatives, each element adds a layer of value to the neighborhood and, by extension, to your investment.

Approaching infrastructure development with a keen eye for detail and a long-term vision will allow you to uncover hidden opportunities in emerging neighborhoods. These insights form the bedrock of informed, strategic investment decisions that can yield significant returns and contribute to sustainable growth.

Remember, the goal is not just to invest in properties but to invest in neighborhoods that are poised for growth. By zeroing in on the various aspects of infrastructure development, you'll be well-equipped to make those winning choices.

Chapter 7:
Risk Management in
Real Estate Investing

Risk management in real estate investing isn't just about avoiding loss; it's about strategically navigating uncertainties to unlock potential gains. You see, balancing your portfolio with a keen eye on diversification strategies can mitigate exposure to market volatility. Legal considerations also play a crucial role, and being proactive about compliance can prevent costly pitfalls down the line. Always stay informed about zoning laws and regulatory changes, as these factors can profoundly affect property values and project feasibility. By integrating these risk management practices, you don't just protect your investments—you position yourself for sustained growth and success in the ever-evolving real estate market.

Diversification Strategies

Diversification in real estate investing is not just a buzzword; it's a critical strategy to mitigate risk and optimize returns. By spreading your investments across various property types, locations, and market conditions, you can protect yourself against market volatility and unexpected downturns. Let's dive into how you can craft a diversified real estate portfolio that'll stand the test of time.

First off, diversification means having a mix of residential and commercial properties. While residential properties like single-family homes and multi-family units provide steady rental income, commercial properties such as office buildings and retail spaces can yield higher returns during favorable economic conditions. But the allure of commercial real estate comes with its unique challenges, such as longer vacancy periods and more complex lease agreements. Balancing both types can smooth out these issues.

Location, location, location—it's not just a catchphrase. Investing in different geographic locations can shield you from regional economic downturns. For instance, economic conditions in the Rust Belt are vastly different to those on the West Coast. By spreading your investments across various states or even countries, you lower the risk of your entire portfolio suffering from localized economic slumps. This geographical diversification provides a cushion against unforeseen market shifts that could otherwise wipe out a less diversified portfolio.

A less talked about yet equally effective diversification strategy is to invest across different market segments. Distinguish between stable, growing, and emerging markets. Stable markets provide predictability and steady returns, while growing markets offer a bit of both security and upside potential. Emerging markets, although riskier, have the potential for significant appreciation. By intelligently allocating your resources across these segments, you can capture a broad spectrum of investment opportunities.

In addition to diversification by property type and location, consider different strategies within the same market. For instance, you might mix long-term buy-and-hold properties with fix-and-flip projects. While fix-and-flips can provide quick returns, they're also subject to higher risk and require more active management. On the other hand, long-term rentals offer passive income and potential for gradual appreciation. Balancing these approaches can give you both immediate gains and long-term stability.

Let's talk about timing. Real estate doesn't move at the same pace across all sectors. Commercial real estate might lag behind residential, or vice versa. Understanding market cycles allows you to time your investments strategically. Diversifying your portfolio to include properties at various stages of their investment cycles can help you stay profitable across different market conditions. Early-stage investments in emerging neighborhoods, for example, can yield high returns as those areas develop and grow. Meanwhile, mature markets provide stability and less volatile returns.

Don't underestimate the importance of various financing methods. Some properties might benefit from traditional mortgages, while others could be better suited for creative financing options like seller financing or hard money loans. Having a mix of financing strategies not only provides flexibility but also leverages your purchasing power, thereby diversifying your risk related to debt obligations.

Investment diversification isn't only about the physical assets; it's also about the financial vehicles you choose. Real Estate Investment Trusts (REITs) offer a way to diversify without directly owning properties. Investing in a mix of publicly traded REITs and private real estate deals can provide liquidity and stability while still capitalizing on property appreciation. REITs are akin to mutual funds, pooling investors' money to invest in a diverse portfolio of real estate assets. This can be an excellent way to get instant diversification if you're short on capital or prefer a more hands-off approach.

Another dimension of diversification lies in asset classes within real estate. Beyond residential and commercial, consider investing in industrial properties, self-storage units, and even specialized niches like student housing or senior living facilities. Each class reacts differently to economic changes, providing another layer of risk management. For example, self-storage units tend to perform well during economic downturns as people downsize and need extra storage space.

Don't forget about the roles of partnerships and syndications in diversification. Partnering with other investors allows you to pool resources, share risks, and access larger or higher-quality properties than you could on your own. Real estate syndications, where multiple investors fund a single large project, offer the chance to diversify into high-value assets like hotels or large apartment complexes without shouldering the entire financial burden.

Technology has also made it easier to diversify your real estate investments. Online platforms now allow you to invest in properties around the world with just a few clicks. These platforms often provide the necessary due diligence, market analysis, and management services, making it feasible to diversify without needing to be an expert in every market you invest in. Leveraging technology can open up new avenues for diversification that were previously inaccessible to individual investors.

Lastly, educational diversification is immensely valuable. Continuously educating yourself on various aspects of real estate investing not only improves your decision-making but also provides you with new strategies to diversify effectively. Attending seminars, reading industry reports, and networking with other investors can introduce you to innovative investment opportunities and diversification techniques that you might not have considered.

In sum, diversification in real estate investing isn't a one-size-fits-all strategy. It requires a thoughtful mix of property types, locations, market segments, investment strategies, financing methods, and even knowledge bases. By weaving these elements together, you create a robust portfolio that is better equipped to withstand market fluctuations and deliver consistent, long-term growth.

Embrace the notion that diversification is not merely about spreading risk but also about strategically positioning yourself to seize opportunities across various spectrums of the market. A well-diversified real estate portfolio is your armor against uncertainty and your ticket to sustainable wealth.

Legal Considerations

The realm of real estate investing is not just shaped by market forces and financial acumen but is also deeply intertwined with a web of legal considerations. For investors, ignorance of the law is not bliss; it's a recipe for potential pitfalls that could undermine their financial goals. Understanding the legal landscape can mean the difference between a successful investment and a costly mistake.

From the outset, engaging in real estate transactions involves multiple layers of legal documentation. Purchase agreements, lease agreements, and disclosure forms are just a few of the documents you will encounter. These documents serve as the blueprint of your rights and obligations. It's vital to meticulously review each clause and condition. For example, failing to understand the contingencies in a purchase agreement could lead to unexpected obligations that can be both inconvenient and costly.

Land use and zoning laws are crucial factors that investors must consider. These regulations determine how a property can be used—whether for residential, commercial, or industrial purposes. Missteps here can be costly. Imagine purchasing a property for what you believe to be a lucrative commercial venture, only to find it's zoned strictly for residential use. Conducting a zoning analysis before acquisition can save you from such costly mistakes.

Another important aspect is compliance with building codes and standards. These laws are designed to ensure safety, health, and welfare within the built environment. They encompass a wide range of elements, from structural integrity to accessibility features. Overlooking these codes can lead to hefty fines, litigation, and even the closure of your property. Therefore, it's crucial to ensure your property adheres to all local, state, and federal building regulations.

An often-overlooked yet critical legal consideration is environmental compliance. Laws related to environmental protection can significantly impact your investment. Factors such as hazardous waste, water quality, and air quality standards can impose constraints on property development and use. If you acquire a property found to be in violation of these regulations, remediation costs can be astronomical. As an investor, commissioning an environmental assessment during the due diligence phase can mitigate these risks.

Real estate taxes are another area that requires close attention. Property taxes can vary significantly based on location, property type, and use. Being aware of potential tax liabilities and opportunities for tax relief is essential. Some jurisdictions offer tax incentives for developing in underserved areas or for making energy-efficient upgrades. Leveraging these incentives can enhance the profitability of your investment.

Investor relations and partnerships also involve legal intricacies. Joint ventures, syndications, and other forms of investment partnerships require detailed agreements outlining the roles, responsibilities, and profit-sharing mechanisms among the parties involved. A well-drafted partnership agreement can prevent disputes and ensure smooth collaborative efforts. Always consider consulting a real estate attorney to draft or review these agreements.

Tenants' rights are another vital consideration, especially for those investing in rental properties. Landlords must navigate federal, state, and local laws governing tenant relations, including lease terms, eviction processes, and habitability standards. Ignorance of these laws can lead to legal battles and financial losses. It is essential to be aware of your obligations and responsibilities as a landlord to avoid legal entanglements.

Insurance requirements form another cornerstone of the legal framework in real estate investing. Property and liability insurance protect you from potential losses due to damages, accidents, or natural disasters. Ensure that the insurance policies you select are comprehensive and tailored to the specific risks associated with your property. Regular reviews and updates to your insurance coverage can safeguard your investment against unforeseen events.

Financing arrangements also come with their own sets of legal considerations. Mortgage agreements, loan covenants, and other financing documents spell out the terms of your financial obligations. Defaulting on a loan can lead to foreclosure, damaging your credit score and financial standing. Carefully reviewing the terms and conditions of financing agreements and maintaining open communication with lenders can prevent financial setbacks.

Finally, intellectual property considerations may come into play, particularly when branding or marketing your real estate investments. Trademarks, service marks, and copyrights protect the unique aspects of your real estate business and marketing materials. Protecting your brand identity can set you apart in a competitive market and provide legal recourse against infringement.

In summary, legal considerations in real estate investing encompass a broad spectrum of issues that are essential to manage effectively. From zoning laws and environmental regulations to tenant rights and financing agreements, the legal landscape can be complex. Nonetheless, staying informed and seeking professional legal advice when necessary can help you navigate these complexities, mitigate risks, and ultimately achieve your investment goals.

Chapter 8:
Financial Analysis and Funding

Jumping into the crux of real estate investment requires more than just a keen eye for emerging neighborhoods; it demands a rigorous financial analysis and strategic funding approach. Assessing property value involves both art and science—balancing market comps, projected rental incomes, and future appreciation potential. Funding, on the other hand, opens a range of avenues from traditional mortgages to creative financing like joint ventures and crowdfunding. Understanding the gamut of financing options available will empower you to seize opportunities swiftly and strategically, maximizing returns while managing risks effectively. Remember, a comprehensive financial blueprint can be the backbone of your investment strategy, driving long-term success in the dynamic landscape of real estate.

Assessing Property Value

One of the most critical steps in your real estate investment journey is assessing property value. Misjudging this can spell disaster, turning potential profits into unavoidable losses. On the other hand, accurately evaluating property value not only sets the stage for sound investment decisions but also helps secure financing, negotiate deals, and anticipate future returns. So how do you go about this task?

While it's tempting to rely solely on gut feeling or general market trends, neither approach offers the accuracy needed for a solid investment strategy. Instead, multiple layers of data and analysis come into play. Begin with a detailed evaluation of comparable properties, or "comps," in the vicinity of your target property. Comps provide a baseline for your assessment by showcasing the selling price of similar properties in similar conditions within the neighborhood.

Next, it's crucial to consider the cost approach, which involves calculating what it would cost to replace or reproduce the property. This method is particularly useful for properties that are unique or have few comparables. The cost approach provides insight into whether the property is overvalued compared to its replacement cost. Coupling this with a market approach ensures that you have a holistic view of the property's value.

The income approach, another essential valuation method, is indispensable when dealing with rental properties or commercial real estate. This approach involves evaluating the potential income the property can generate, thus providing a value that's more aligned with its earning potential. Essentially, this method offers insights into the property's long-term profitability based on its net operating income (NOI).

Yet, all these traditional methods have their limitations. That's why integrating technology can give you an edge. Advanced algorithms and AI-driven platforms can offer predictive analytics, helping you gauge future property values based on an array of market conditions, including demographic shifts, economic trends, and regulatory changes. Using tools like automated valuation models (AVMs) can supplement your traditional valuation methods, making your assessment even more robust.

It's essential to consider external factors that could affect property value. Market conditions, economic indicators, and geopolitical events can all have significant impacts. For instance, economic downturns can lead to decreased property values, while infrastructure development can boost them. Stay updated with fiscal policies and local government plans that could influence property dynamics, such as new public transit routes or zoning changes.

Location remains paramount in assessing property value. The neighborhood's safety, proximity to amenities like schools, healthcare facilities, and shopping centers play a crucial role. Future growth prospects, usually gauged through demographic trends, can suggest whether a location's value will appreciate. For example, an influx of younger professionals into an area typically indicates good rental income prospects.

Don't overlook the physical condition of the property. Take note of the structural integrity, age of key installations like HVAC systems, and the condition of the roof or foundation. Beyond visible aspects, consider hidden factors like plumbing, electrical wiring, and insulation. An in-depth property inspection will reveal potential future costs that might affect your investment calculations. Additionally, consider the potential costs of necessary renovations or improvements that can uplift the property value.

Market sentiment can also be a powerful, often underestimated, predictor of property values. Sentiment is shaped by a combination of media reports, public perceptions, and investor chatter. Understanding and sometimes even anticipating market sentiment can offer opportunities to buy undervalued properties or sell overvalued ones before general consensus catches up.

Financing mechanisms also play a role in assessing property value. If you're using loans, the interest rates and terms of those loans will affect your calculations of the property's worth. A higher interest rate could decrease your profit margins, while favorable loan conditions could make a property more attractive and vice-versa. Thus, aligning your financing strategy with your property evaluation is vital.

The condition of the broader economy can't be ignored either. Economic indicators such as employment rates, GDP growth, and consumer spending levels should influence your assessments. Steady economic growth typically signals increased property values, while economic downturns may necessitate more conservative estimates.

Regulatory and tax environments can have nuanced yet profound impacts on property value. For example, changes in property taxes, capital gains tax, or even changes in rental property regulations can either enhance or diminish property value. Stay abreast of any planned changes in these areas to adjust your valuations accordingly. Understanding the local government's stance on development and incentives can also provide insights.

It's also wise to consider environmental factors, both immediate and long-term. Properties situated in areas prone to natural disasters or those close to sources of noise pollution generally have lower values. Conversely, properties near parks or water bodies often see higher valuations. With growing awareness about environmental sustainability, energy-efficient properties or those adapted to green building standards can fetch a premium.

Many investors make the mistake of neglecting future value potential. This involves not just looking at current valuation but how it's likely to change over time. To do this effectively, consider trends in urbanization, technological advancements, and social behaviors. An area that's not particularly valuable today could turn into a lucrative investment tomorrow if you anticipate these changes accurately.

Let's not forget the role of professional appraisals. While personal assessments are crucial, professional appraisers offer an unbiased valuation, ensuring that you're making decisions based on impartial data. These experts use a combination of methods we've discussed, along with industry experience, to provide a comprehensive value assessment.

In the end, assessing property value is more of an art than a science. It requires blending quantitative data with qualitative insights. It demands a deep understanding of market dynamics, an eye for potential, and a grasp of economic indicators. By mastering the intricacies of property valuation, you'll be well on your way to making informed, profitable investment decisions.

Remember, every piece of data and every insight counts in this domain. The more thorough your evaluation, the lesser the risk and the higher the rewards. As you fine-tune your skills, you'll find that assessing property value becomes second nature, empowering you to seize opportunities that others might overlook.

Financing Options

In the realm of real estate, one of the most crucial elements for success is securing the right financing. The paths to financial backing for property investment are numerous and varied, making it essential to understand the landscape. Whether you're an experienced investor or a novice, knowing your financing options can mean the difference between a profitable venture and a missed opportunity.

First off, let's explore traditional bank loans. Banks offer a variety of mortgage options tailored to meet different financial circumstances and investment goals. Conventional mortgages are a popular choice, often characterized by their competitive interest rates and defined payment schedules. These loans typically require a substantial down payment, generally around 20%. This makes them particularly appealing to those with significant initial capital.

On the other hand, let's discuss Federal Housing Administration (FHA) loans. These are designed for individuals who may not have the substantial down payments that conventional loans demand. With FHA loans, down payments can be as low as 3.5%, making property investment more accessible. However, the trade-off is often in the form of mortgage insurance premiums that can add to the overall cost of the loan.

For those seeking flexibility, adjustable-rate mortgages (ARMs) offer an intriguing avenue. Unlike fixed-rate mortgages, the interest rates on ARMs vary over the loan's life, which can be beneficial if you anticipate a decline in rates or plan to sell or refinance before the rate adjusts significantly. It's crucial to weigh the risks with this type of loan, as rising interest rates can increase your monthly payments unexpectedly.

Beyond traditional avenues, there are private loans from non-bank lenders and private investors. This category includes hard money loans, typically short-term and secured by the property itself. These loans are more expensive, with higher interest rates and closing costs, but they provide faster access to capital and require fewer formalities. They can be a lifeline for investors needing quick financing, particularly in competitive markets where time is of the essence.

Moreover, let's not overlook the potential of crowdfunding platforms in today's digital age. Crowdfunding pools small investments from a large number of people, making significant capital available for real estate projects. This democratizes access to real estate investment opportunities, opening the door to those who might not have the means to go it alone. While this method offers less risk concentration for investors, it often comes with its own set of regulatory requirements and platform fees.

Another modern financing method comes in the form of Real Estate Investment Trusts (REITs). Through REITs, individual investors can purchase shares in commercial real estate portfolios that receive income from a variety of properties. This not only spreads the risk but also allows for liquidity, as shares can typically be bought and sold like stock. Although REITs demand a stringent adherence to regulatory standards, their benefits can be substantial for the right investor.

Furthermore, let's address the potential of seller financing. In this arrangement, the seller essentially acts as the lender, offering financing directly to the buyer. This can be particularly advantageous in markets where traditional lending options might be scarce or for buyers looking to avoid the rigorous qualification processes typical of conventional loans. It provides both parties with greater flexibility in negotiating terms that work mutually.

For seasoned investors or those involved in larger projects, syndication offers a compelling opportunity. Through syndication, a lead investor or sponsor partners with a group of investors to pool resources and share the profits and risks. This strategy enables access to larger properties and higher-value investments that might otherwise be unattainable for an individual investor. Effective syndication requires meticulous legal and financial structuring but can yield significant returns.

Additionally, don't forget about government and municipal grants and loans. Various federal, state, and local programs are designed to spur investment in underserved or emerging neighborhoods. These programs can offer low-interest loans, tax incentives, or even outright grants to qualifying investors. While jumping through bureaucratic hoops can be a challenge, the financial benefits can be significant. Investigating such opportunities often requires thorough research and sometimes specialized knowledge or partnerships.

If you're looking to take on commercial properties, commercial mortgages are worth considering. These are designed specifically for income-generating properties such as retail spaces, office buildings, and multi-family units. Commercial mortgages usually require a larger down payment and involve more stringent qualifications compared to residential loans. However, they offer the benefit of being tailored to the income potential of the property, making them an integral part of any serious investor's toolkit.

We also can't ignore the role of venture capital. While more commonly associated with tech startups, venture capital firms are increasingly venturing into real estate, especially for projects with high-growth potential. Venture capital can provide substantial funding, but it often comes at the cost of giving up some control and equity. This type of financing works best for ambitious, large-scale projects where the potential rewards justify the relinquished shares and control.

For those intent on long-term growth, home equity loans or lines of credit (HELOCs) offer another financing option. Leveraging the equity in an existing property can provide the down payment or renovation funds needed for a new investment. HELOCs are particularly appealing due to their revolving credit nature, although it's essential to carefully consider the risks, as your primary home serves as collateral.

Lastly, don't underestimate the importance of personal savings and retirement accounts like a Self-Directed IRA (SDIRA). Investing through an SDIRA allows you to use retirement funds to purchase real estate while enjoying tax benefits. While this requires careful management to comply with IRS rules, the long-term benefits can bolster your investment portfolio substantially.

- Conventional Mortgages: Great for those with strong credit and significant down payments.

- FHA Loans: Accessible option for those with lower down payments.

- Adjustable-Rate Mortgages (ARMs): Offers flexibility but comes with potential risks.

- Private Loans and Hard Money Loans: Quick and less formal but more expensive.

- Crowdfunding: Democratizes investment opportunities, though it includes platform fees.

- REITs: Offers liquidity and risk spreading, suitable for stock market investors.

- Seller Financing: Flexible and negotiable, ideal for markets with limited traditional options.

- Syndication: Great for large projects, pooling resources and sharing risks.

- Government and Municipal Loans: Offers low-interest options but requires thorough research.

- Commercial Mortgages: Tailored for income-generating properties, requiring larger down payments.

- Venture Capital: Suitable for high-growth projects, though it may require giving up control.

- Home Equity Loans and HELOCs: Useful for leveraging existing property value.

- Personal Savings and SDIRAs: Ideal for long-term growth with tax benefits.

Navigating through these financing options can seem overwhelming, but the key lies in thoroughly understanding each and determining which aligns best with your investment strategy. The right financing can propel your real estate ventures, enabling you

Chapter 9:
Building a Real Estate Investment Portfolio

Constructing a real estate investment portfolio requires a strategic mix of properties that maximize returns and mitigate risks over the long haul. It's not just about buying a few properties and hoping for the best; you need a clear vision and a diverse strategy. Imagine your portfolio like a well-balanced diet, diversified between residential units, commercial spaces, and perhaps even some industrial properties. Balancing high-risk, high-reward investments with stable, income-generating ones can ensure consistent growth and financial security. Start by identifying your investment goals: Are you focusing on capital appreciation, steady rental income, or a combination of both? Once your goals are clear, leverage market trends and data to pinpoint prime investment opportunities. Continually reassess your portfolio to weed out underperforming assets and reinvest in high-potential properties. Remember, building a robust portfolio is a dynamic process that requires ongoing learning, flexibility, and strategic planning.

Long-Term Growth

Long-term growth in real estate investment isn't just about acquiring property and waiting. It's about strategic planning, active management, and a keen eye on market trends. In the volatile world of property investments, it's easy to get swayed by short-term gains. But true wealth is built by those who keep their eyes on the far horizon, focusing on sustainable growth over decades.

One of the most critical elements of long-term growth is understanding and leveraging appreciation. Real estate appreciates over time, but this isn't a given—it's a calculated risk. Properties tend to gain value due to factors like location improvements, economic growth in the area, and demand for housing. Smart investors pinpoint these growth areas by conducting comprehensive market analysis and staying updated on urban development plans and policy changes.

Diversification plays a huge role in managing the risk associated with long-term investments. By spreading investments across different property types, such as residential, commercial, and mixed-use properties, and across multiple neighborhoods or cities, investors can protect themselves against market fluctuations. Even within real estate, you can diversify further by considering different building ages, tenant types, and lease terms.

The concept of **forced appreciation** can significantly aid long-term growth. Unlike natural appreciation, forced appreciation involves proactive improvements to a property that increase its value. These might include renovations, adding amenities, or converting unusable space into rentable areas. By upgrading properties, investors not only increase rental income but also the resale value of the property.

Cash flow management is another cornerstone of long-term growth. Positive cash flow means the properties generate more income than the expenses involved in holding them. This ongoing income stream allows investors to reinvest in their portfolio, either by paying down debts faster or by accumulating capital to purchase additional properties. Consistently reevaluating cash flow and making adjustments as needed helps to maintain a healthy, robust portfolio.

Financing strategies also play a crucial role in the long-term growth of a real estate portfolio. Understanding various financing options, from traditional mortgages to creative financing methods like seller financing, lease options, or using private investors, enables investors to stretch their capital further and potentially leverage other people's money to grow their portfolio.

Next, keeping an eye on market cycles can make a huge difference. Real estate markets are cyclical, with periods of boom and bust. Understanding where we are in the cycle can inform investment strategies. For instance, during a market downturn, acquiring properties at a discount can position an investor well for when the market rebounds. In a hot market, it might be wiser to focus on cash flow properties instead of betting on appreciation.

Tenant retention is often overlooked in long-term real estate strategies but can be a game-changer. High tenant turnover can eat into profits, thanks to vacancy periods and the costs associated with finding new tenants. Creating a positive tenant experience through excellent property management, responding promptly to maintenance requests, and fostering a sense of community can lead to long-term leases and stable income.

Another vital factor is automation and leveraging technology. As an investor, your time is precious. Technologies like property management software, automated rent collection systems, and even AI-driven market analysis tools can save countless hours and provide accurate, up-to-date data to inform your decisions. Technology not only streamlines operations but can also offer deeper insights into market trends and property performance.

Building relationships is essential for long-term success. Networking with other real estate professionals, attending industry events, and being active in real estate investment groups can open doors to new opportunities, provide valuable insights, and offer support. Mentorship from seasoned investors can also provide guidance and help you avoid common pitfalls.

Environmental sustainability and social responsibility are becoming increasingly important in real estate investment. Properties that adhere to green building standards and employ sustainable practices tend to attract higher-quality tenants and can command premium rents. Moreover, investing in properties that have a positive community impact contributes to long-term growth and brand reputation.

Mental resilience and patience can't be understated. Real estate investments might not always yield immediate results, and it's those who stay committed through the ups and downs who ultimately see the most benefits. Keeping focused on the long-term vision can help maintain motivation and prevent rash, short-sighted decisions.

"The journey of a thousand miles begins with a single step." This wisdom resonates profoundly when we consider the realm of real estate investment for long-term growth. Every property purchase, every tenant relationship, every market analysis incrementally builds towards substantial financial freedom and legacy.

In conclusion, building a real estate investment portfolio for long-term growth involves an intricate dance of strategic planning, market knowledge, financial acumen, and ongoing management. By focusing on appreciation, diversification, cash flow, tenant retention, leveraging technology, and fostering strong relationships, investors can build a robust portfolio that stands the test of time. Real estate, when approached with a long-term mindset, becomes not just a means of income but a pathway to enduring wealth and lasting impact.

Portfolio Balance

Balancing your real estate portfolio is as much an art as it is a science. To craft a well-diversified and balanced portfolio, you need a strategic approach that takes into account various asset classes, risk tolerance, and investment goals. Whether you're a seasoned investor or just starting, achieving the right balance can enhance returns and mitigate risks, ensuring long-term growth.

At its core, portfolio balance in real estate involves the distribution of investments across different types of properties and geographic locations. This strategy isn't about random diversification; rather, it's about making calculated choices that align with market trends, personal financial goals, and potential growth areas. Think of it as assembling a puzzle where each piece must contribute to the overall picture of financial stability and growth.

Start by assessing your risk tolerance and investment horizon. Are you looking for stable, long-term income or quick, high returns? Your answer will guide your asset allocation. For instance, high-risk, high-reward investments might include emerging neighborhoods or under-developed properties that have potential for significant appreciation. Conversely, low-risk investments often involve established neighborhoods with steady rental incomes.

Balance isn't just about the types of properties you invest in but also their locations. Geographic diversification is crucial. This involves investing in various markets to protect your portfolio from local economic downturns. For example, if you have several properties in one city, a local economic slump could drastically impact your returns. By spreading investments across different regions, you shield your portfolio from localized risks.

Residential properties, commercial real estate, and mixed-use developments each offer unique advantages and risks. Residential properties, like single-family homes or multi-family units, usually provide stable income and less volatility but may grow at a slower rate. On the other hand, commercial properties, such as retail spaces or office buildings, can offer higher returns but come with higher risks, especially related to tenant defaults or vacancies during economic downturns.

A balanced portfolio often includes a mix of both residential and commercial properties. This blend ensures you capitalize on steady residential rental incomes and the superior appreciation potential of commercial real estate. Consider the current economic environment, demographic shifts, and urban development plans when making these investment choices.

Another aspect of maintaining portfolio balance is aligning your properties' growth stages. Properties at different stages of development or appreciation can provide a more cohesive strategy for constant income and capital growth. For instance, investing in some newly built properties alongside older, well-established ones can give a balance of immediate income and future appreciation.

Additionally, consider the liquidity of your investments. Real estate is traditionally not a liquid asset, but having some properties that are easier to sell or refinance can help in times of need. Including investments like Real Estate Investment Trusts (REITs) can add this liquidity component to your portfolio, allowing for easier access to funds without the lengthy process of selling property.

Funding options can also impact portfolio balance. Leveraging different types of financing can help diversify your risk. Using a mix of loans, personal equity, and even partnerships can offer different financial benefits and risks. For instance, while loans may increase leverage and potential returns, they also come with higher risks if market conditions sour.

Regularly reviewing and rebalancing your portfolio is essential to maintaining its health. Market conditions change, and so do investment opportunities. Regular assessment allows you to prune non-performing assets and reallocate resources to more promising ventures. This dynamic approach to portfolio management ensures you remain agile and prepared to adapt to changing market landscapes.

Remember, the goal is to create a portfolio that not only meets your current financial needs but also positions you strongly for future growth. Real estate investment is a long-term commitment, and strategic portfolio balance is crucial in navigating the highs and lows of economic cycles.

In summary, a balanced real estate portfolio can provide the stability and growth needed to build lasting wealth. By diversifying across property types, locations, and funding options, you create a resilient investment strategy. Regular reassessment and strategic planning will keep your portfolio aligned with your long-term goals, ensuring that you're well-prepared for whatever the future holds.

Chapter 10:
The Role of Technology in Real Estate

In today's fast-paced world, technology is revolutionizing the real estate industry, providing investors with powerful tools to make informed decisions and optimize their portfolios. From advanced market research tools that crunch data and offer insights in real-time, to property management software that streamlines operations and tenant communications, tech advancements are reshaping traditional real estate practices. Savvy investors can leverage these technologies to gain a competitive edge, identifying profitable opportunities with greater precision and mitigating risks through data-backed strategies. As the digital landscape continues to evolve, those who embrace these innovations stand to benefit significantly, driving growth and achieving long-term success in an increasingly dynamic market.

Market Research Tools

The transformative impact of technology on real estate cannot be overstated, especially when it comes to market research. Investors today have access to an array of tools that can provide crucial insights into market trends, property values, and neighborhood dynamics. These tools help investors make informed decisions and minimize risks. By leveraging these technologies, you can unlock new levels of profitability in real estate investments.

Data analytics platforms are at the forefront of these technological advancements. These platforms aggregate vast amounts of data from diverse sources such as property listings, demographic statistics, crime rates, and economic indicators. One such tool is Zillow, which provides robust data insights on property values, rental prices, and market trends. By analyzing this information, investors can identify patterns and predict future market movements, allowing for smarter investment strategies.

Advanced Geographic Information Systems (GIS) offer spatial analysis capabilities that go beyond simple mapping. They reveal comprehensive neighborhood insights, from traffic patterns to environmental risks. Tools like Esri's ArcGIS help pinpoint areas experiencing significant infrastructural developments, thereby highlighting emerging neighborhoods worth investing in. The visual component of GIS also makes it easier to present data to stakeholders, ensuring everyone is on the same page.

Artificial Intelligence (AI) and Machine Learning (ML) algorithms are reshaping market research. These technologies can process enormous datasets quickly and identify trends and anomalies that would be difficult for humans to detect. AI-driven tools such as HouseCanary and Reonomy use sophisticated algorithms to offer precise property valuations and market forecasts. This gives investors a competitive edge by enabling more accurate prediction models and risk assessments.

Subscription-based platforms like CoStar and REIS offer exhaustive market analytics and benchmarking data. These platforms provide high-quality reports and insights into various property sectors, including residential, commercial, and industrial real estate. They also offer trend analysis, economic forecasts, and competitive intelligence, making them invaluable for detailed market research.

Often overlooked but highly valuable are social media analytics tools. Social media platforms like Facebook, Twitter, and LinkedIn are abundant sources of real-time data about local sentiment, emerging trends, and public opinion. Tools like Hootsuite and Brandwatch allow you to track mentions, hashtags, and trending topics that could signal shifts in neighborhood desirability or property value. This real-time feedback can be a goldmine for investors looking to stay ahead of market movements.

Public records and government databases are essential, yet traditional sources of market research data. Websites like the U.S. Census Bureau and local municipal databases provide invaluable demographic information, zoning regulations, and property tax details. Although more manual than automated analytics platforms, they are irreplaceable for validating other data sources and ensuring a comprehensive understanding of the market.

Virtual and Augmented Reality (VR and AR) technologies are bringing a new dimension to market research. Investors can now virtually tour properties and neighborhoods without leaving their desks. Platforms like Matterport offer 3D virtual tours that give an in-depth view of properties, including the minute details often missed in photos or videos. AR apps like Homesnap allow investors to walk through neighborhoods virtually and get real-time information about properties for sale, including their history and comparables.

Blockchain technology is emerging as a promising tool in real estate market research. Platforms like Propy and Ubitquity are pioneering the use of blockchain for secure and transparent property transactions and records. This technology not only ensures data integrity but also democratizes access to information, making market research more reliable and accessible.

For those looking to delve deeper into financial analytics, software suites such as Argus and RealData offer advanced tools for cash flow analysis, investment modeling, and property valuation. These platforms are indispensable for investors who want to conduct thorough financial due diligence. By using customizable models and "what if" scenarios, you can better anticipate potential returns and risks, thus making more informed investment decisions.

Finally, technology also enables real-time field data collection. Mobile apps like SiteSeer and LandGrid allow investors to collect, store, and analyze field data on the go. Whether it's taking notes during property visits, capturing photos, or tagging locations, these apps ensure you never miss critical on-site details. This data can then be integrated with other analytics platforms for a more holistic market analysis.

The rise of automated valuation models (AVMs) is another game-changer in market research. AVMs use statistical modeling to value properties based on various data points such as recent sales, property characteristics, and market conditions. For instance, tools like Redfin Estimate and CoreLogic's RealAVM provide quick and reliable property valuations, allowing you to make faster investment decisions.

Cloud computing platforms are also playing a crucial role by providing scalable storage and computing power for massive datasets. Solutions like Google Cloud and Amazon Web Services (AWS) offer secure and scalable environments for running complex market analyses and data visualizations. These platforms support advanced analytics and machine learning models, giving investors the computational power required for in-depth research.

When it comes to assessing economic trends and indicators, macroeconomic tools like Bloomberg Terminal and Trading Economics offer unparalleled insights. These platforms provide real-time updates on economic indicators that can significantly impact real estate markets. Factors like interest rates, employment rates, and GDP growth can be continuously monitored to better time your investments.

For collaborative research, platforms like Google Workspace enable real-time collaboration and data sharing among team members. Google Sheets and Google Data Studio, for example, can help create dynamic dashboards and reports, allowing for collaborative analysis and decision-making. This collaborative approach ensures that everyone involved in the investment process has access to the latest data and insights.

Ultimately, the wealth of market research tools available today equips investors with unprecedented levels of information and analytics capabilities. These tools not only make it easier to identify high-potential investment opportunities but also enable you to manage risks more effectively. By harnessing these technologies, you can turn data into actionable insights, paving the way for more strategic and profitable real estate investments.

Property Management Software

In today's fast-paced real estate market, staying ahead of the competition means leveraging every tool available, and property management software is one such tool. This technology has revolutionized the way investors, property managers, and landlords handle their assets. From automating routine tasks to providing real-time data, property management software has transformed property management from a time-consuming chore into an efficient and streamlined process.

One of the primary benefits of property management software is its ability to automate repetitive and mundane tasks. Things like rent collection, tenant screening, maintenance scheduling, and even lease management can be managed through a single platform. For instance, automated rent reminders reduce the chances of late payments, while online payment systems make it convenient for tenants and ensure funds are transferred rapidly. This level of automation frees up time for property managers to focus on more strategic activities, such as identifying new investment opportunities or improving tenant relationships.

But automation isn't the only advantage. Property management software also provides comprehensive data analytics capabilities. With access to detailed financial reports, occupancy rates, and maintenance logs, property managers can make informed decisions that drive profitability. Real-time insights allow for better financial planning and risk management. By spotting trends early, managers can proactively address potential issues, whether they be maintaining property value or identifying a dip in tenant satisfaction.

Tenant experience is another crucial area that benefits immensely from using property management software. User-friendly portals allow tenants to easily submit maintenance requests, pay their rent online, and access important documents. Seamless communication between landlords and tenants fosters a positive relationship and can lead to higher tenant retention rates. In an industry where keeping your tenants happy directly impacts your bottom line, this technological edge cannot be overstated.

For property managers handling multiple properties, the software can drastically simplify operations. Centralized dashboards provide a holistic view of all assets, allowing for quick comparison and analysis. This unified approach is particularly useful for investors and developers who need to track different property types, from single-family homes to extensive multi-family units. The software can handle the nuances of managing diverse property portfolios, whether they are scattered across different cities or concentrated in one region.

Data security should not be overlooked either. Modern property management software is designed with robust security features to protect sensitive information. From encrypted transactions to secure access controls, these platforms ensure that both tenant and owner data remain confidential and safe from breaches. This trust is paramount, especially in an era where data privacy regulations are becoming increasingly stringent.

Additionally, integrating property management software with other technological tools amplifies its effectiveness. For instance, combining it with advanced market research tools can offer comprehensive insights into market trends and property performance. Integration with CRM (Customer Relationship Management) systems can enhance tenant engagement strategies. Leveraging IoT (Internet of Things) devices, property managers can monitor property conditions in real time, enabling predictive maintenance and reducing operational costs.

Another often underappreciated aspect of property management software is its role in optimizing marketing efforts. The software can track and analyze marketing campaign performance, pinpoint the most effective channels, and help property managers refine their strategies. Automated listings can keep vacancies low by ensuring properties are advertised promptly and across multiple platforms. Comprehensive tenant databases can also be leveraged for targeted marketing, making outreach efforts more efficient and personalized.

Legal compliance is yet another area where property management software shines. Keeping up with ever-changing regulations can be daunting, but built-in compliance tools ensure that all lease agreements, tenant screening procedures, and rent transactions adhere to local and federal laws. This minimizes the risk of legal disputes and fines, providing peace of mind to property managers and investors alike.

Moreover, the reporting features offered by property management software are invaluable for financial planners and accountants. Detailed financial reports, including income statements, balance sheets, and cash flow reports, are generated effortlessly. These reports provide a clear picture of a property's financial health, aiding in budget planning, tax preparation, and financial forecasting. The ability to segregate income and expenses by property is crucial for investors managing diverse portfolios, allowing for precise ROI calculations.

When it comes to scalability, property management software excels. Whether you are managing a handful of properties or expanding to a nationwide portfolio, the software can adapt to your growing needs. Customizable features and modules allow you to scale operations without the need for significant changes or additional staffing. This scalability makes it a particularly attractive option for aspiring investors looking to streamline their entry into the market and experienced professionals seeking to expand their holdings.

In terms of cost-efficiency, while there might be an initial investment in acquiring property management software, the return on investment is significant. Reduced labor costs, lower vacancy rates, and improved maintenance efficiency can result in substantial savings over time. Additionally, the automation of various processes decreases the likelihood of human error, further enhancing cost-effectiveness.

Investors and property developers who have adopted property management software often report greater satisfaction, improved tenant relationships, and increased profitability. As technology continues to evolve, the capabilities of these platforms will only expand, offering even more sophisticated tools to navigate the complexities of real estate investment and management.

To sum up, property management software is not just a convenience—it's a necessity for a modern, efficient, and profitable real estate operation. Its ability to streamline operations, enhance tenant experiences, provide crucial insights, and ensure legal compliance makes it an indispensable tool for anyone serious about maximizing their real estate investments.

Chapter 11:
Real Estate Investment Trusts (REITs) and Emerging Neighborhoods

Real Estate Investment Trusts (REITs) offer a sophisticated yet accessible way to dive into the world of real estate, providing a channel for investors to gain from diverse property portfolios without the complexity of direct ownership. In emerging neighborhoods, REITs play a pivotal role in capitalizing on growth opportunities while managing risks. Whether it's commercial spaces or residential developments, these trusts pool resources to invest in high-potential areas, enabling investors to benefit from rental income and property value appreciation. Understanding REIT investment strategies can be your key to unlocking substantial returns. By examining REIT structures and focusing on market-specific dynamics, you can align with macroeconomic trends and capture the upward trajectory of emerging neighborhoods. This chapter will guide you through mastering REITs as a powerful tool for seizing opportunities and navigating the real estate landscape effectively.

Understanding REITs

Real Estate Investment Trusts (REITs) have emerged as a popular vehicle for both seasoned and new investors to gain exposure to the real estate market without the need for direct property ownership. Understanding how REITs operate and their potential benefits can empower investors to make informed decisions and diversify their portfolios effectively.

At its core, a REIT is a company that owns, operates, or finances income-producing real estate. Unlike traditional real estate investments, REITs offer a unique blend of liquidity and dividends. They allow investors to purchase shares in a trust that directly invests in real estate properties, such as office buildings, shopping centers, apartments, and hotels. By law, REITs must distribute at least 90% of their taxable income to shareholders in the form of dividends, making them an attractive option for income-seeking investors.

- There are three main types of REITs: Equity REITs, Mortgage REITs (mREITs), and Hybrid REITs. Equity REITs are the most common, dealing with owning and operating income-producing real estate. They generate revenue primarily through leasing space and collecting rents on the properties they own over long-term. Mortgage REITs, on the other hand, provide financing for income-producing real estate by purchasing or originating mortgages and mortgage-backed securities. Hybrid REITs combine the investment strategies of both equity and mortgage REITs.

- Equity REITs are typically more stable and less sensitive to interest rate changes compared to mREITs. Investors looking for regular income payouts and long-term growth often lean toward Equity REITs. Mortgage REITs might appeal to those seeking higher dividend yields, albeit with greater interest rate risk. Understanding these differences is crucial for aligning REIT investments with personal financial goals and risk tolerance.

Additionally, REITs are required to abide by real estate regulations and tax rules that are unique to their structure. For instance, REITs benefit from not paying corporate tax if they comply with specific distribution and organizational requirements. This tax advantage allows

REITs to offer attractive dividend yields compared to other investments, like bonds or stocks.

The accessibility of REITs makes them an appealing choice for investors who wish to gain exposure to the real estate market without the
complexities of direct property investment. Shares of publicly traded
REITs can be bought and sold on major stock exchanges, offering liquidity that direct property ownership cannot match. This liquidity is
beneficial for investors who need to reallocate their portfolios quickly
in response to market changes. Furthermore, there are non-traded and
private REITs, though these often come with different risk and liquidity profiles.

Investing in REITs also provides diversification advantages. Real
estate has historically shown a low correlation with other asset classes,
such as stocks and bonds. By including REITs in a diversified portfolio, investors can potentially reduce overall portfolio risk and volatility.
This aspect of REIT investing can't be understated, particularly in the
context of market downturns.

Moreover, REITs can serve as a hedge against inflation. Real estate
values and rents tend to rise with inflation, so REITs can provide a
measure of protection in inflationary periods. The tangible nature of
property, combined with the income from rents and long-term appreciation potential, gives REITs an edge in preserving value over time.

For those focusing on emerging neighborhoods, REITs can be an
essential tool. Emerging neighborhoods often come with increased potential for property value appreciation as new developments and infra-
structures attract residents and businesses. REITs that focus on these
areas can provide exposure to these growth opportunities without the
need for direct property management. This allows investors to capitalize on neighborhood growth trends effectively.

It's important to dive deeper into the various sectors within REITs. Some REITs specialize in residential properties, while others focus on commercial, industrial, or specialized sectors like healthcare or logistics. Each of these sectors comes with its own set of risks and rewards. For instance, residential REITs might offer more stability, while commercial REITs could offer higher growth potential. Understanding these nuances can aid investors in selecting the right type of REIT for their specific investment strategy.

When considering REIT investments, it's crucial to analyze the management team behind the REIT. The success of a REIT often hinges on the expertise and experience of its managers. A reputable management team with a strong track record can navigate market cycles and make strategic property acquisitions that add significant value over time. Therefore, due diligence is essential before committing capital to a REIT.

Moreover, the financial health of a REIT is another critical factor. Key financial metrics such as Funds From Operations (FFO), Adjusted Funds From Operations (AFFO), and net asset value (NAV) provide insights into a REIT's performance and valuation. Investors should scrutinize these metrics to ensure the REIT's income sources are sustainable and its properties are appreciating.

Another advantage of REITs is their requirement to disclose financial information publicly. This transparency enables investors to make informed decisions based on detailed financial reporting and property information. However, like any investment, REITs are not without risks. Market conditions, interest rate fluctuations, and regulatory changes can impact REIT performance. This necessitates a keen understanding of broader economic and property market trends.

Furthermore, some emerging neighborhoods might have specific REITs focused on their development, providing targeted investment opportunities. These REITs can be particularly attractive as they often align with government incentives and infrastructure projects that spur growth. Investing in these REITs can provide a strategic advantage by positioning ahead of broader market recognition.

For those just starting out, REITs can serve as a graceful entry into real estate investing. With lower initial capital requirements compared to purchasing property outright, REITs democratize access to real estate's income and growth potential. They allow novice investors to learn the ropes of real estate investment, diversify their holdings, and gain exposure to professional management practices.

In conclusion, understanding REITs requires no less diligence than direct property investment but offers numerous benefits such as liquidity, diversification, and income potential. By grasping how REITs operate, evaluating their financial health, and recognizing their strategic placement in emerging neighborhoods, investors can harness their power to build long-term wealth. Whether you're a seasoned investor or just beginning your real estate journey, REITs represent a dynamic and accessible way to invest in the ever-evolving real estate market. Through informed decisions, strategic positioning, and ongoing market analysis, investors can effectively use REITs to unlock the manifold opportunities presented by emerging neighborhoods.

REIT Investment Strategies

Investing in Real Estate Investment Trusts (REITs) can be an effective gateway into the realm of property investment, particularly when zeroing in on emerging neighborhoods. These communities, often overlooked yet brimming with potential, offer unique opportunities for substantial returns. Diving into REITs centered on these areas requires a blend of strategic thinking, in-depth analysis, and a robust understanding of market trends.

First and foremost, understanding the distinct categories of REITs is paramount. Publicly traded REITs offer liquidity akin to stocks, whereas non-traded REITs generally involve longer-term commitments but may lead to higher returns. When pinpointing emerging neighborhoods, both types could provide strategic advantages. Public REITs enable quick adjustments to your investment portfolio in response to market shifts. In contrast, non-traded REITs might offer early access to high-potential properties before they hit the mainstream market.

When it comes to leveraging REITs in emerging neighborhoods, geographical diversification is a critical tactic. Spreading investments across various up-and-coming areas mitigates risks tied to hyper-local downturns. For example, if one neighborhood experiences slower growth due to unforeseen developments, another burgeoning area in a different part of the city or country could offset those losses.

Additionally, it's crucial to consider the type of properties held within the REIT. Some REITs focus on residential properties, such as single-family homes or multi-family units. Others might invest in commercial real estate like retail spaces and office buildings. Each property type can perform differently depending on the neighborhood's development stage. Mixed-use properties often hold particular promise in emerging areas, spearheading urban revitalization while attracting both residents and businesses.

Understanding the macroeconomic factors driving growth in these neighborhoods is also essential. Factors such as job growth, infrastructure projects, and population trends heavily influence a neighborhood's trajectory. A strategic approach involves investing in REITs that target areas benefiting from these drivers. For instance, a neighborhood earmarked for a new tech hub or significant public transportation upgrade might witness rapid appreciation in property values.

Timing plays a pivotal role in REIT investment strategies within emerging neighborhoods. Early entry during the nascent stages of a neighborhood's development can yield exponential gains as the area matures. However, this requires diligent research and sometimes a bold willingness to take calculated risks. Once a neighborhood starts gaining traction, it's vital to continuously monitor ongoing developments and market conditions to determine the right moment for rebalancing your investments.

Active monitoring and management further enhance the effectiveness of a REIT strategy. Regularly reviewing quarterly earnings reports, staying abreast of market trends, and even visiting the neighborhoods can offer invaluable insights. Moreover, leveraging technology and real estate analytics tools can refine your investment choices, enabling more precise predictions about future growth and profitability.

While many investors focus on large, metropolitan markets, some of the most lucrative REIT opportunities lie in secondary or tertiary markets. These markets often get overshadowed by major cities but harbor neighborhoods on the cusp of transformation. These hidden gems can be included in a diversified REIT portfolio, balancing the stability of more established markets with the high-growth potential of emerging communities.

Another critical strategy involves understanding the tax implications linked to REIT investments. REITs must distribute at least 90% of their taxable income to shareholders as dividends, which are often taxed at a higher rate than long-term capital gains. Therefore, integrating tax-efficient investment vehicles such as IRAs or 401(k)s might amplify overall returns.

Regulatory aspects also play a significant role in shaping REIT strategy. Favorable zoning laws, tax incentives, and government-backed initiatives can accelerate growth in emerging neighborhoods, making them more attractive to REITs. Staying informed about policy changes and legislative updates can position investors to capitalize on these benefits. For example, a neighborhood slated for rezoning to accommodate higher-density residential projects might present substantial opportunities for growth-oriented REITs.

Beyond financial considerations, socially responsible investing is becoming increasingly relevant. Investing in REITs that emphasize sustainability, community development, and ethical practices can not only yield financial returns but also contribute positively to the neighborhoods. These investments often align with broader market trends towards ESG (Environmental, Social, and Governance) criteria and may appeal to investors seeking to balance profit with purpose.

Collaborating with real estate professionals, such as brokers and developers in emerging neighborhoods, can offer an edge. These experts possess localized knowledge and insights that might not be readily available through standard market reports. Building relationships with these professionals can provide early access to lucrative opportunities, helping investors get ahead of market trends.

Lastly, flexibility and adaptability underpin successful REIT investment strategies. The real estate market is inherently dynamic, with emerging neighborhoods evolving at different paces. Being willing to reassess and adjust your strategy in response to market shifts, economic indicators, and emerging trends ensures sustained growth and mitigates potential risks.

In conclusion, crafting a winning REIT strategy in emerging neighborhoods involves a blend of geographical diversification, understanding the drivers of growth, meticulous timing, active management, tax considerations, regulatory awareness, and socially responsible investing. By integrating these elements, investors can maximize their returns while contributing to the sustainable development of burgeoning communities. Through strategic and informed REIT investments, emerging neighborhoods can turn into thriving markets, creating a win-win scenario for both investors and communities alike.

Chapter 12:
The Impact of Government Policies

Government policies have a profound influence on real estate investment, shaping markets in ways both overt and subtle. By understanding zoning laws, regulations, and tax incentives, investors can tap into lucrative opportunities that might otherwise go unnoticed. For instance, favorable zoning changes can transform underutilized areas into sought-after investment hotspots, while tax credits for developments in designated zones can significantly boost returns. Conversely, stringent regulations can constrain property use and stymie growth if not properly navigated. Hence, staying informed about policy shifts and legislative trends isn't just advisable—it's essential for anyone aspiring to build a resilient and profitable real estate portfolio. Strategically leveraging governmental frameworks allows investors to mitigate risks, optimize performance, and ultimately gain an edge in the dynamic landscape of emerging neighborhoods.

Zoning and Regulation

In the labyrinth of real estate investing, government policies, especially zoning and regulation, are pivotal. They have the power to make or break investment opportunities. Zoning laws, by dictating the types of buildings that can be constructed in specific areas, define the landscape of possibilities. Understanding these nuances is an essential skill for any savvy investor.

Zoning impacts how land can be used—whether for residential, commercial, industrial, or mixed-use purposes. Local governments establish these regulations to foster organized development, ensure safety standards, and balance the varied needs of a community. For investors, this means navigating the complex web of zoning laws can either uncover hidden advantages or pose substantial hurdles.

Consider the potential development of a new residential complex. If the area is zoned exclusively for single-family homes, pursuing a multi-family unit investment will be futile unless the zoning laws are changed. Conversely, if an area is rezoned to allow for higher density residential buildings, it could present lucrative opportunities to tap into growing housing demands.

Zoning laws can influence not just the types of buildings, but also their heights, bulk, and distances from property lines. For commercial real estate, aspects such as parking regulations, signage restrictions, and even aesthetic guidelines must be adhered to. These layers of regulation ensure harmonious growth but require investors to be astutely aware of local guidelines and future zoning changes.

One of the critical aspects of zoning is the concept of "upzoning" and "downzoning". Upzoning involves changing the zoning classification to allow for higher density or more intensive use of the property, which can significantly enhance property value and investment potential. Downzoning, on the other hand, reduces the allowable density or limits the potential uses for a property, often to preserve the character of a neighborhood or to address environmental concerns. Investors who can anticipate or influence such zoning changes stand to gain considerably.

It's crucial to recognize that zoning laws aren't static. They evolve with policy shifts, community needs, and urban development plans. Hence, an investor's success often hinges on staying informed about proposed zoning changes and participating in local planning meetings. Being proactive in these discussions can offer strategic advantages, potentially allowing investors to shape policy to their benefit.

Moreover, zoning isn't merely a regulatory concern; it's also a reflection of community aspirations. Communities use zoning laws to promote specific social, economic, and environmental goals. For instance, some cities are adopting "inclusionary zoning" policies that mandate a certain percentage of new residential projects must be affordable housing. While such regulations might initially seem restrictive, they can also open doors to incentives like density bonuses or expedited permitting processes, making projects financially viable.

Furthermore, the intricacies of zoning include variances and special exceptions. A variance allows property owners to deviate from specific zoning requirements, often granted when strict enforcement would cause unnecessary hardship due to unique property conditions. Special exceptions allow for permissible uses that are not explicitly allowed under current zoning laws. These mechanisms provide investors with the flexibility to navigate through restrictive zoning landscapes and capitalize on opportunities that might otherwise be inaccessible.

Investors must also be vigilant about overlay districts. These are special zoning districts layered over existing ones, imposing additional restrictions or providing incentives to achieve specific planning objectives, such as historic preservation or environmental protection. Overlay districts can complicate the development process but can also offer unique investment opportunities aligned with public policy goals.

One can't discuss zoning without touching on the role of zoning boards and planning commissions. These bodies oversee the application of zoning laws, approve variances and special exceptions, and shape the future urban landscape. Being familiar with the visions and priorities of these entities can provide insights into upcoming zoning changes and development trends.

Zoning laws have a profound impact on land values. Properties that align with the highest and best use per zoning regulations often command premium prices. Conversely, properties rendered less valuable due to restrictive zoning can present opportunities for shrewd investors who can navigate the path to rezoning or adapt the property to permissible uses creatively.

It's equally important to understand the potential for zoning conflicts and legal challenges. Disputes over zoning decisions can lead to protracted legal battles, affecting project timelines and profitability. Investors need to factor in such risks and engage legal experts when navigating contentious zoning landscapes.

When considering investments in emerging neighborhoods, due diligence on zoning laws is non-negotiable. Conducting a zoning analysis involves not just reviewing current regulations but also understanding the zoning history, pending zoning applications, and the master plan guiding future developments. This holistic overview helps in predicting the trajectory of neighborhood growth and aligning investment strategies accordingly.

Zoning laws are instrumental in guiding urban development but can also be leveraged to create value. Smart investors recognize the importance of zoning as a tool to maximize returns while adhering to legal frameworks. By masterfully navigating zoning regulations, engaging with community planning processes, and anticipating shifts in zoning policies, investors can unlock the full potential of their real estate ventures in emerging neighborhoods.

Tax Incentives and Credits

In the realm of real estate investment, one of the most powerful tools at an investor's disposal is tax incentives and credits. Governments at various levels, from federal to local, often use tax policies to stimulate economic growth, especially in emerging neighborhoods. These incentives can significantly enhance the financial viability of investment projects and offer strategic advantages that can propel wealth-building efforts.

Tax incentives come in many forms, including deductions, exemptions, abatements, and credits. Each serves a unique purpose, directly impacting an investor's bottom line. For instance, tax credits reduce your tax liability on a dollar-for-dollar basis, which can be incredibly beneficial for bigger projects with substantial costs. On the other hand, deductions lower your taxable income, thus reducing the tax you owe.

Let's take a closer look at some of the common tax incentives and credits available to real estate investors. The Federal Historic Preservation Tax Incentives program is a prime example. This program offers a 20% income tax credit for the rehabilitation of historic, income-producing buildings. It's a win-win situation: preserving architectural gems while benefiting financially. This doesn't just apply to historic downtown areas; many emerging neighborhoods contain historic structures that are ripe for such opportunities.

Local governments often have their own sets of incentives aimed at revitalizing neighborhoods. Tax Increment Financing (TIF) is one widespread mechanism used to encourage investment. TIF districts are designed to capture future increases in property taxes to fund current improvements. By reinvesting the increased tax revenues into infrastructure and public projects, these districts make the area more attractive for further private investment. Simple urban upgrades can transform the appeal of a previously overlooked area.

Enterprise Zones are another initiative worth discussing. These zones are specific geographic areas designated by governments to infuse economic prosperity into lagging regions. Investors in enterprise zones often receive a variety of tax benefits, including property tax abatements and income tax credits. These incentives make it easier to justify investments in areas that may initially seem high-risk but have great potential for appreciation.

Moreover, Opportunity Zones, introduced under the Tax Cuts and Jobs Act of 2017, have become a focal point for savvy investors.

These zones are distressed areas identified by the government where investments can be made with significant tax advantages. Investors can defer capital gains taxes by reinvesting those gains into Opportunity Funds, which are then used to finance projects within Opportunity Zones. The potential for a high ROI, alongside the tax benefits, makes Opportunity Zones extremely appealing.

The Low-Income Housing Tax Credit (LIHTC) is another significant incentive for real estate investors, particularly those interested in multifamily developments. LIHTC aims to encourage the development of affordable housing by offering tax credits to developers. These credits can be sold to private investors, providing immediate equity to developers, which in turn lowers their project's overall debt. The stabilization of rental income streams and the societal impact of increasing affordable housing stock add both financial and ethical valor to such investments.

When thinking about tax incentives and credits, it's crucial to consider renewable energy incentives. Installing renewable energy systems like solar panels can qualify property owners for federal tax credits, often coupled with local and state incentives. These not only reduce energy costs but also enhance the property's value, making it more attractive to eco-conscious tenants or buyers. In an increasing number of emerging neighborhoods, sustainability is more than a trend; it's a demand driver that attracts both residents and commercial tenants.

Navigating these incentives requires due diligence and often expert advice. It's essential to work closely with tax professionals who are experienced in real estate. They can help you identify which incentives you qualify for and how best to apply them to your investment strategy. Properly structured deals can lead to substantial savings and improved cash flow, a cornerstone for long-term success in real estate.

Another aspect to consider is that many of these incentives require compliance with certain conditions and regular reporting. For example, LIHTC projects must maintain specific occupancy levels of low-income tenants to benefit from the credits. Staying compliant not only ensures continued receipt of tax benefits but also protects the investment from potential legal issues.

Capitalizing on tax incentives and credits isn't just about short-term gains. Strategic use of these tools can contribute to sustained profitability and wealth accumulation. By reducing the overall cost burden of investments, you can allocate more resources toward expanding your portfolio, exploring new ventures, or improving existing properties. This is especially crucial in emerging neighborhoods, where the initial investment risk may be higher but the long-term returns can be lucrative.

As we continue to witness shifts in economic and social landscapes, government policies are likely to evolve. Staying informed about these changes can offer new opportunities or necessitate shifts in strategy. For instance, new policies aimed at promoting green buildings, tech hubs, or cultural districts can open the door to untapped incentives that weren't previously available.

To sum up, tax incentives and credits are indispensable in the toolkit of a real estate investor. They provide the leverage needed to maximize profitability while mitigating risks. Aspiring and seasoned investors alike should pay close attention to these financial instruments, staying proactive, informed, and aligned with evolving policies. When used effectively, tax incentives and credits can transform the way you approach real estate investments, turning calculated risks into rewarding ventures.

In conclusion, understanding and leveraging tax incentives and credits is more than just an added benefit; it's a strategic imperative. Whether you're interested in residential properties, commercial spaces, or mixed-use developments, these incentives can propel your projects from merely viable to highly profitable. As you master the art of investing in emerging neighborhoods, always keep an eye on how tax strategies can enhance your returns and drive forward your investment goals.

Chapter 13:
Social Responsibility and Community Impact

In the realm of real estate investing, social responsibility and community impact are more than just buzzwords; they are critical components for sustainable success. Ethical investing isn't simply about feeling good—it's about generating lasting value that supports community development and fosters strong, thriving neighborhoods. Entrepreneurs and investors have the unique opportunity to enhance community value by creating quality housing, supporting local businesses, and ensuring inclusive growth. This thoughtful approach not only builds goodwill but also establishes a solid foundation for long-term profitability. When you invest in a way that uplifts communities, you're not just making a financial commitment—you're building a legacy that reflects integrity, promotes social equity, and encourages a cycle of positive economic impact. Everyone benefits from this synergy, from residents to investors, making it a cornerstone strategy for any forward-thinking real estate professional.

Ethical Investing

Investing in real estate is not just about generating high returns, accumulating wealth, or achieving financial freedom. There's a growing movement that emphasizes the importance of aligning investment strategies with ethical considerations. This concept, widely known as ethical investing, is crucial for those who want their financial activities to have a positive impact on society and the community.

At its core, ethical investing involves making investment decisions that reflect a set of moral principles. For real estate investors, this means considering the broader implications of their actions on the environment, society, and governance structures, often referred to as ESG criteria. Ethical investors take into account factors that go beyond financial metrics to ensure their investments contribute to the public good.

One key element of ethical investing is environmental sustainability. Real estate investors should prioritize eco-friendly building practices and energy-efficient properties. This could involve investing in buildings that use renewable energy sources, comply with green building standards like LEED certification, or incorporate sustainable materials in construction. Not only do these practices benefit the environment, but they can also be attractive to tenants and buyers who are increasingly eco-conscious.

Another aspect is social responsibility. Investors should think about how their investments affect local communities. Redeveloping a neighborhood shouldn't lead to the displacement of existing residents; rather, it should aim to enhance the area and provide opportunities for everyone. This might mean engaging with community leaders, supporting local businesses, or investing in affordable housing projects. These efforts can help foster a sense of community and contribute to long-term neighborhood stability.

Governance is the third pillar of ethical investing. This involves ensuring transparency, accountability, and fairness in business operations and investment practices. Real estate investors should perform due diligence to avoid engaging with partners and contractors involved in unethical practices, such as labor exploitation or corruption. Ethical governance can lead to more sustainable, reliable, and ultimately profitable investments.

The importance of ethical investing extends to risk management as well. Properties that adhere to ESG criteria are often more resilient to market fluctuations and regulatory changes. For example, buildings that meet high environmental standards may face fewer regulatory hurdles in the future, protecting investors from sudden compliance costs. Meanwhile, socially responsible investments may benefit from community support, reducing risks related to vacancy and tenant turnover.

Achieving ethical investing isn't just about avoiding negative impacts; it's also about creating positive ones. Investors can drive social change by deliberately choosing projects that address societal challenges. For example, financing developments in under-served areas can provide much-needed services like healthcare, education, and grocery stores, which can uplift entire communities.

Although the primary goal for many investors is profitability, ethical investing shows that making money and doing good are not mutually exclusive. Indeed, properties designed with ESG principles often command higher valuations and attract more reliable tenants, who are drawn to spaces that mirror their values. Ethical investing can lead to not just financial returns but also sustainable, long-term community benefits.

It's also essential to recognize the growing demand for socially responsible investing. Public awareness around issues such as climate change, social justice, and corporate governance is at an all-time high. Investors who can demonstrate a commitment to ethical principles are likely to attract more interest from a broader base of stakeholders, including tenants, buyers, and financial partners. Increasingly, consumers and businesses prefer to engage with like-minded entities, and this trend is only expected to rise.

To incorporate ethical investing into your real estate strategy, start by setting clear goals that align with your values. This might involve prioritizing green buildings, committing to fair labor practices, or ensuring that your investments contribute to community development. Conduct thorough research to understand the impact of your investments and engage with stakeholders to get a complete picture of how your projects will affect the local area.

Furthermore, consider using ethical investment frameworks and guidelines such as the United Nations Principles for Responsible Investment (UNPRI) or the Global Reporting Initiative (GRI). These frameworks provide comprehensive guidelines for incorporating ESG criteria into investment strategies, offering practical tools and benchmarks to help measure and improve ethical impact.

Another strategy is to engage in impact investing, which explicitly aims to generate positive, measurable social or environmental impacts alongside a financial return. In real estate, impact investing might encompass affordable housing projects, developments in blighted areas, or properties that offer essential services to under-served communities. Impact investing goes hand in hand with ethical investing, as it prioritizes long-term benefits over short-term gains.

Finally, investors should be prepared to lead by example. Ethical investing offers an opportunity to set standards in the industry, encouraging peers to adopt similar practices. By showcasing successful ethical investments, you can inspire others to consider the broader implications of their financial decisions and contribute to a more responsible investment environment. Your actions can serve as a template for those looking to balance profit with purpose.

In conclusion, ethical investing is more than a trend; it's a paradigm shift in how we think about wealth and its impact on the world. For real estate investors, incorporating ethical principles into investment strategies means considering the long-term effects on the environment, society, and governance. By making conscientious choices, investors not only foster sustainable communities but also set the stage for enduring financial success.

Enhancing Community Value

Enhancing community value is not just a buzzword in the sphere of real estate investment; it is a foundational principle for creating sustainable and profitable investment opportunities. When investors inject capital into emerging neighborhoods, the ripple effects extend far beyond the financial spreadsheets.

To grasp how community value is enhanced, one must first understand the intrinsic connection between real estate development and social responsibility. Real estate investments, particularly in emerging neighborhoods, have the potential to revitalize entire communities. Investment isn't just about buildings and structures; it's about forging stronger, more resilient neighborhoods that benefit all stakeholders, from residents to local businesses.

Let's start with economic stimulation, which is one of the most immediate ways real estate investments can enhance community value. When investors focus on emerging neighborhoods, they often promote job creation and boost local economies. Whether it's through the construction phase or ongoing property management, new projects require manpower and resources. Local vendors, contractors, and service providers see a surge in demand, catalyzing economic growth on multiple fronts.

Furthermore, enhancing community value transcends economic metrics. Social benefits emerge through improved amenities and services. Imagine transforming a derelict lot into a vibrant community center or park. Such developments provide residents with spaces to gather, socialize, and engage in recreational activities. This fosters a sense of belonging and ownership, as people are more likely to invest in the upkeep and overall well-being of their neighborhoods when they have access to quality communal spaces.

Educational facilities are another critical aspect. Investors keen on long-term success often participate in the development or improvement of schools and educational programs. Quality education creates pathways for economic mobility and helps retain families within these emerging neighborhoods. Schools frequently act as a barometer of neighborhood desirability, directly impacting property values and community stability.

Health is another dimension where community value can be significantly enhanced. By partnering with local health care providers, investors can help establish clinics and wellness centers. Accessible health care reduces absenteeism in workplaces and schools, enhances productivity, and significantly improves the quality of life for residents. A healthier community is a more stable and attractive one, appealing to both current and prospective residents.

Public safety improvements can't be overlooked, either. Investment in emerging neighborhoods often includes enhancing public safety measures, whether through better lighting, security systems, or collaborative efforts with local law enforcement. Safer neighborhoods tend to see reduced crime rates, which boosts investor confidence and attracts other stakeholders to join in the revitalization efforts.

Investing in infrastructure is also a surefire way to enhance community value. Improvements in roads, public transportation, and utilities not only make neighborhoods more livable but also more attractive for future investment. Infrastructure development serves as the backbone of community growth, providing the necessary support for both residential and commercial projects. Improved infrastructure can reduce traffic congestion, lower carbon footprints, and even contribute to a better overall quality of life.

Art and culture are other pillars often revitalized through real estate investments. By incorporating art installations, cultural centers, and performance spaces, investors can breathe new life into an area. These elements add a unique character to neighborhoods, making them more appealing and culturally rich. Art and culture not only beautify areas but also provide platforms for community engagement and social cohesion.

Environmental sustainability should not be overlooked. Modern real estate investments often include green building practices and sustainability measures. From energy-efficient buildings to sustainable landscaping, these investments reduce the community's ecological footprint. Sustainable neighborhoods are not only more attractive to environmentally conscious residents but also tend to have lower long-term operational costs.

Of course, enhancing community value also involves listening to the current residents and adapting investments to meet their needs. Open forums, town hall meetings, and surveys can provide invaluable insights. Community engagement ensures that developments are in line with local needs and actually benefit those who live there. This participatory approach can significantly increase the chances of project success and community acceptance.

Another essential facet of enhancing community value is fostering local entrepreneurship. Real estate investments can provide affordable retail and office spaces for local businesses. Supporting small businesses not only diversifies the local economy but also creates unique neighborhood identities that attract residents and visitors alike. Entrepreneurial hubs and incubators are examples of initiatives that can transform emerging neighborhoods into thriving economic and social ecosystems.

Moreover, understanding and respecting the historical and cultural context of a neighborhood can enhance its value. Revitalization efforts should aim to preserve the unique heritage and historical landmarks of a community. This generates a sense of pride among residents and makes neighborhoods distinct and attractive. Heritage conservation combined with modern development creates a harmonious blend of the old and new, leading to enriched community value.

Community value is not just a byproduct but a strategic element of successful real estate investments. While investors focus on financial returns, it is crucial to recognize that these returns are intimately linked with the broader well-being of the community. As the real estate maxim goes, location is everything, and a high-value, thriving community is the ultimate location for sustainable, profitable investments.

In sum, enhancing community value involves a multi-faceted approach that includes economic stimulation, social development, public safety, infrastructure improvements, cultural enrichment, environmental sustainability, and community engagement. These elements work synergistically, creating a virtuous cycle where the enhanced value of the community feeds back into higher property values and more attractive investment opportunities. By adopting a holistic investment strategy that prioritizes community value, investors are not only placing themselves in the path of profitable returns but also contributing to the creation of sustainable and resilient neighborhoods.

Online Review Request for This Book

If this book has provided you with valuable insights into profitable real estate investment and effective community enhancement, please consider leaving an online review to help others discover and benefit from these strategies.

Building a Legacy
Through Smart Investments

Congratulations! You've journeyed through an extensive wealth of knowledge that covers the ins and outs of investing in emerging neighborhoods. By now, you understand the significance of strategic, well-informed decisions in achieving long-term financial success. But it's essential to consider what truly lies at the core of these investments—building a legacy.

What does it mean to build a legacy? It's more than just accumulating wealth. It's about creating a lasting impact that transcends generations. Smart investments pave the way for financial freedom, but they also contribute to the growth and development of communities. They have the power to catalyze change, enrich lives, and set an enduring precedent for future investors.

Let's begin by reflecting on the knowledge you've garnered in this book. From understanding the dynamics of emerging markets to analyzing neighborhood potential and managing risks, each chapter has equipped you with the tools to navigate the complex world of real estate investment. The principles you've learned are the bedrock upon which your legacy will stand.

Consider the importance of identifying and seizing opportunities in residential properties. Single-family homes and multi-family units offer myriad possibilities for growth and revenue generation. Your investments in these areas can revitalize neighborhoods, increase housing availability, and foster a sense of community. The ripples of such investments can lead to enhanced local infrastructure, better schools, and improved quality of life.

Commercial real estate presents another lucrative avenue. Retail spaces and office buildings are not just income-producing assets; they are essential to the economic fabric of any community. When you invest in these properties, you're supporting local businesses, creating jobs, and stimulating economic growth. It's about envisioning the broader impact your investments can have, beyond just financial returns.

The role of technology in real estate cannot be overstated. Leveraging advanced market research tools and property management software can streamline your operations, improve efficiency, and maximize profits. Staying ahead of technological trends ensures that your investments remain competitive and sustainable. It's about embracing innovation to build a future-ready portfolio.

A well-diversified investment portfolio is crucial to mitigating risks and ensuring steady growth. As we've discussed, diversification across property types, locations, and investment vehicles can provide a balanced approach to wealth creation. It's the smart management of your investments that will ensure their resilience in the face of market fluctuations. A diverse portfolio is a fortress against economic uncertainties, safeguarding your legacy for future generations.

Financial analysis and funding are critical components of any successful investment strategy. Assessing property value accurately and securing the right financing options are foundational steps. The ability to analyze and interpret financial data will empower you to make informed, strategic decisions. Remember, building a legacy involves not just acquiring assets but nurturing them for sustained growth.

The impact of government policies, from zoning regulations to tax incentives, plays a significant role in shaping the real estate landscape.

Being well-versed in these areas will enable you to capitalize on opportunities and navigate potential pitfalls. Informed investors can leverage policy changes to their advantage, ensuring that their investments remain compliant and profitable.

Investing with social responsibility in mind is not just a moral imperative; it is a strategy that enhances community value. Ethical investing ensures that your financial gains do not come at the expense of others. It's about creating win-win scenarios where both investors and communities thrive. This approach fosters goodwill, community support, and a positive reputation, all of which are integral to building a lasting legacy.

A Vision for the Future

Envision the transformative power of your investments. Picture emerging neighborhoods blossoming into thriving communities with bustling commercial centers, well-maintained residences, and robust infrastructure. See children playing in safe, vibrant parks, families accessing quality education and healthcare, and local businesses flourishing. Your investments can be the catalyst for this change, driving economic growth and social upliftment.

Your journey as an investor doesn't end here. It's a continuous process of learning, adapting, and evolving. The real estate market is dynamic, and staying informed is key. Engage with the latest market trends, participate in industry forums, and leverage professional networks to stay ahead. This proactive approach will ensure that your legacy remains relevant and impactful.

Moreover, consider mentoring aspiring investors and sharing your insights. Knowledge transfer is a powerful tool in creating a lasting legacy. By guiding others, you amplify the positive impact of your investments, fostering a community of informed, responsible investors.

Your legacy thus extends beyond your financial success, influencing and inspiring future generations.

In conclusion, building a legacy through smart investments is about more than just financial acumen. It requires a holistic approach that includes market analysis, strategic planning, risk management, and ethical considerations. It's about understanding the broader picture—how your investments shape communities, influence lives, and create lasting value.

As you move forward, remember that each investment decision you make is a brushstroke on the canvas of your legacy. Paint wisely, with vision and purpose, and the result will be a masterpiece that stands the test of time. Happy investing!

Appendix A:
Case Studies of Successful Emerging Neighborhood Investments

Throughout this book, we've explored strategies, analyzed data, and discussed the critical factors that make emerging neighborhoods prime candidates for investment. Now, let's delve into real-world examples that put these concepts into action. These case studies highlight how investors identified opportunities, managed risks, and ultimately reaped substantial rewards. Each story serves as a testament to the power of strategic planning and market insight.

Case Study 1: The Revival of East Austin, Texas

Once overlooked, East Austin transformed dramatically over the last decade. Investors began to spot the area's potential as the city experienced significant economic growth and demographic shifts.

- **Initial Challenges:** High crime rates and a lack of infrastructure made initial investments risky.

- **Strategic Entry:** Early investors focused on undervalued residential properties and small commercial spaces.

- **Key Drivers of Growth:** Proximity to downtown Austin, inflow of tech companies, and a youthful, creative population.

- **Outcome:** Property values quadrupled within ten years, turning initial investments into substantial profits.

This case underscores the importance of timing and recognizing the impact of macroeconomic trends on local markets.

Case Study 2: The Renaissance of Detroit's Midtown

Detroit's Midtown offers another powerful example. Despite the city's financial struggles, investors saw potential in its rich cultural history and strategic location.

- **Initial Challenges:** High vacancy rates and widespread urban decay.

- **Strategic Entry:** Focused on multi-family units and partnerships with local organizations for renovation projects.

- **Key Drivers of Growth:** Investment in arts and education, local government incentives, and collaborative community projects.

- **Outcome:** A thriving neighborhood with high occupancy rates, increased rental income, and a rejuvenated community spirit.

This example illustrates the transformative power of community involvement and public-private partnerships.

Case Study 3: The Upswing of Pittsburgh's Lawrenceville

Lawrenceville in Pittsburgh shifted from an industrial bastion to a vibrant, trendy neighborhood. Here's how it happened:

- **Initial Challenges:** Deindustrialization had left many properties vacant and neglected.

- **Strategic Entry:** Investors targeted old warehouses and factories for conversion into lofts and mixed-use developments.

- **Key Drivers of Growth:** Proximity to major universities and healthcare institutions, along with Pittsburgh's broader economic revitalization.

- **Outcome:** Residential and commercial properties saw a massive appreciation, and the area became a magnet for young professionals and entrepreneurs.

This case shows how leveraging existing but underutilized assets can catalyze neighborhood transformation.

Case Study 4: The Rise of Wynwood, Miami

Wynwood was once an area marked by industrial usage but has since become a cultural and artistic hub, thanks to visionary investors.

- **Initial Challenges:** Industrial zoning and lack of residential amenities.

- **Strategic Entry:** Investors focused on converting warehouses into art galleries and creative spaces.

- **Key Drivers of Growth:** Strong arts and cultural scene, city zoning changes that allowed mixed-use development, and increased tourist interest.

- **Outcome:** Skyrocketing property values and a neighborhood that attracts both tourists and residents alike.

Wynwood exemplifies the importance of adapting investment strategies to leverage cultural and regulatory shifts.

Case Study 5: The Flourishing of Nashville's Germantown

Germantown evolved from a historic district to one of Nashville's most sought-after neighborhoods for both living and working.

- **Initial Challenges:** Preservation restrictions and initial resistance from long-term residents.

- **Strategic Entry:** Investment in boutique hotels and upscale dining establishments to attract a higher-income demographic.

- **Key Drivers of Growth:** Nashville's booming music and entertainment industry, strategic city planning, and incentives for historic preservation.

- **Outcome:** High return on investments and a unique blend of historic charm and modern amenities.

This case highlights the potential for blending historical preservation with modern development to create unique investment opportunities.

These case studies illustrate that successful investments in emerging neighborhoods require a mix of vision, strategic action, and an understanding of broader market forces. By learning from these examples, you can identify and capitalize on the next wave of emerging neighborhood opportunities.

Glossary of Real Estate Investment Terms

In this glossary, you'll find key terms and concepts essential for mastering real estate investment. These definitions will help both new and seasoned investors to navigate the complex landscape of emerging markets.

Absorption Rate

The rate at which available properties in a specific market are sold during a given period. It's a critical indicator of market demand.

Appraisal

An expert's estimate of a property's market value, often required by lenders before approving a mortgage.

Asset Management

The process of maximizing a real estate investment's value through strategic management and decision-making.

Capital Expenditures (CapEx)

Funds used by a company to acquire, upgrade, and maintain physical assets such as property or industrial buildings.

Cash Flow

The net amount of cash being transferred into and out of a real estate investment. Positive cash flow indicates that the income generated from a property is greater than the expenses.

Comparative Market Analysis (CMA)

An evaluation tool that helps to estimate a property's value by comparing it to similar properties that have recently sold in the same area.

Debt-to-Income Ratio

The percentage of a borrower's monthly gross income that goes toward paying debts. Lenders use this ratio to assess a borrower's ability to manage monthly payments and repay debts.

Due Diligence

A comprehensive appraisal of a real estate investment, including an examination of financial records and physical inspections, conducted before finalizing the transaction.

Equity

The difference between the market value of a property and the amount owed on any mortgages or liens. It represents the owner's interest in the property.

Fixed-Rate Mortgage

A mortgage with an interest rate that remains constant throughout the term of the loan. It provides budget stability due to predictable monthly payments.

Gross Rent Multiplier (GRM)

A simple method to estimate the value of an income-producing property. It is calculated by dividing the property's price by its gross rental income.

Interest-Only Loan

A type of mortgage where the borrower pays only the interest for a set period. After the interest-only period, they must begin repaying the principal.

Internal Rate of Return (IRR)

A metric used in real estate investment analysis to estimate the profitability of potential investments. It calculates the rate at which the net present value of all cash flows from a property equals zero.

Leverage

Using borrowed capital to increase the potential return on investment. In real estate, leverage can amplify both gains and risks.

Loan-to-Value Ratio (LTV)

A financial term used by lenders to express the ratio of a loan to the value of an asset purchased. It helps to assess the risk of a particular loan.

Net Operating Income (NOI)

The total income a property generates, minus operating expenses, but before interest and taxes. It's a key indicator of a property's profitability.

Real Estate Investment Trust (REIT)

A company that owns, operates, or finances income-producing real estate. REITs provide a way for investors to earn a share of the income produced through commercial real estate without actually having to buy, manage, or finance any properties themselves.

Return on Investment (ROI)

A measure used to evaluate the efficiency of an investment. It is calculated by dividing net profit by the initial investment cost.

Zoning

Municipal or local government regulations that dictate how real estate in specific areas can be used. Zoning laws can impact property values and development potential.

Understanding these terms is fundamental to mastering real estate investment. Knowledge not only empowers but also opens doors to greater opportunities and long-term success.

Appendix B:
Resources for Further Research

To truly master the art of real estate investing in emerging neighborhoods, continuous learning is crucial. This appendix provides you with a curated list of resources to help you deepen your understanding, stay current with industry trends, and refine your investment strategies.

Books

- *The Intelligent Investor* by Benjamin Graham - A classic text providing timeless strategies for value investing.

- *Rich Dad Poor Dad* by Robert T. Kiyosaki - Offers insights into building wealth through smart investing and financial literacy.

- *Building Wealth One House at a Time* by John Schaub - Focuses on real estate investment strategies tailored for long-term growth.

Industry Publications

- *Real Estate Investment Digest* - Features market trends, investment strategies, and expert opinions.

- *Urban Land Magazine* - Published by the Urban Land Institute, provides insights into urban development and real estate investment.

- *REIT Magazine* - Offers comprehensive coverage on Real Estate Investment Trusts and market analysis.

Online Courses and Webinars

- MIT Real Estate Management Program - Offers in-depth courses designed to equip you with advanced skills in real estate investment.

- Udemy Real Estate Investing Courses - A variety of courses covering everything from the basics to advanced investment strategies.

- BiggerPockets Webinars - These webinars cover a range of topics from beginner to expert level real estate investing in a community-driven format.

Websites and Blogs

- *BiggerPockets* - A comprehensive platform offering forums, guides, and tools specifically tailored for real estate investors.

- *Investopedia* - Provides a wealth of information on financial concepts, real estate investing, and market trends.

- *NerdWallet* - Features articles, reviews, and advice on various aspects of real estate investing.

Podcasts

- *BiggerPockets Real Estate Podcast* - Expert interviews and discussions on a variety of real estate investing topics.

- *The Real Estate Guys Radio Show* - Focuses on investment strategies, market insights, and real estate economics.

- *Old Dawg's REI Network* - Offers tips and tricks for older investors looking to build wealth through real estate.

Professional Associations

- *National Association of Realtors (NAR)* - Provides resources, networking opportunities, and market data for real estate professionals.

- *Urban Land Institute (ULI)* - A global organization offering knowledge, research, and networking for urban real estate development.

- *Real Estate Investment Network (REIN)* - Delivers education, market analysis, and networking opportunities for real estate investors.

Government and Regulatory Bodies

- *U.S. Department of Housing and Urban Development (HUD)* - Offers a variety of research reports, market data, and policy updates.

- *Federal Housing Finance Agency (FHFA)* - Provides housing market reports, data, and regulations impacting real estate investments.

- *Internal Revenue Service (IRS)* - Essential for understanding tax codes, incentives, and credits related to real estate investing.

By leveraging these resources, you'll be well-equipped to navigate the complexities of real estate investing in emerging neighborhoods. Keep learning, stay informed, and continually adapt your strategies to build sand maintain long-term wealth.